— *The* —

# PASSIVE
## INCOME
## PHYSICIAN

*The*

# PASSIVE
# INCOME
# PHYSICIAN

## SURVIVING A CAREER CRISIS
## BY EXPANDING NET WORTH

## THOMAS BLACK, MD

**The Passive Income Physician**
**Surviving a Career Crisis by Expanding Net Worth**

ISBN: 978-0-692-82740-6

FIRST EDITION

# Dedication

To ...

Micaela, my wife and soulmate. Without your endless support, none of my personal achievements or our vivid dreams would be possible. You have given me the world and my love for you is eternal.

Evan, Chayse, Charlee and Karsyn. May you follow your dreams and let nothing stand in your way.

Tim and Jen. Your zest for life and your kids is infectious. When I am with you I become the best version of myself.

Teri and Mark. Thank you for the love and generosity you have shared over the years, and the inspiration to reach for new possibilities.

Mom and Dad. You raised us all to be fierce competitors while also sharing your talent for deep love.

# Table of Contents

# The Passive Income Revelation

As a former banker with years of real estate lending experience, I watched many of my clients grow wealthy, but it didn't happen because they bought and then sold property for a profit.

What was it that made them multimillionaires?

Their commercial rental properties reaped large amounts of passive income.

Do you know what passive income is?

I didn't, not at first—or at least I did not fully comprehend its power. It took time for me to realize that the recurring cash they received every month, without fail, was passive, that it was not based on the number of hours they worked at a job. It just kept coming, kept piling up, even while they slept.

Fortunately, I also had another realization. After about a decade of assisting and observing hundreds of clients, it dawned on me that while most were intelligent and hardworking individuals, they were no smarter than me. Certainly, none of them knew more about multifamily financing than I did. That was *my* expertise, even if it had not yet become my road to abundance.

When I read *The Passive Income Physician*, I smiled, because the author's revelations were so similar to my own. We both woke up, learned new skills, then trusted that the same laws that were making other people very wealthy would also work for us. We went from earning six-figure annual incomes to exponentially expanding our net worth and, finally, to being able to provide the kind of financial security many people only dream of.

Nothing ventured, nothing gained, though, right? Of course we had to accept some risk and continue educating ourselves.

That is precisely why Thomas Black's book is so important. By sharing his own story, this emergency medicine physician lays out a blueprint for how you—a highly educated, well-paid but overworked professional—are uniquely qualified to enjoy the same gains. The secret is transitioning your highly taxed earned income to tax-advantaged passive income. Once that happens, you can begin buying back the most precious asset we all have in common: our time and freedom. About six years ago, I decided I was tired of being on the wrong side of every transaction. Some bankers feel powerful doling out loans. In truth, it finally dawned on me that it was far more lucrative to be a borrower than a lender, so I took action.

Despite working a full-time job with a large national bank, I started investing in single-family rental properties, just like Thomas did. Over a two-year period, I acquired fifteen rental houses. Also like my colleague, I soon realized that it was not the type of real estate plan that could be easily scaled up, something Thomas explains quite clearly in this wonderful book. All I had really accomplished was to buy myself a second job. My only choice, then, was to take more action. In 2013, while still employed by the bank and still managing my rental properties, I decided to start syndicating much larger multifamily properties. Again, this book will explain what syndicating is all about. In a nutshell, it basically means raising money and using it to buy real estate. I partnered with one of my clients, and in less than a year, we acquired four apartment complexes, a total of 800 units. The vast majority of the money came from our various equity partners. That's syndicating, and what a concept it is!

It did not take long for me to sell all my rental houses, quit my day job, and go full time into the multifamily business. Subsequently, in the past four years I have led groups that have acquired over 20 properties and over 4,000 apartment units. That's a lot of passive income, folks, a mountain of wealth distribution.

The message is clear: If Thomas and I can do it, so can you. There are no feasible excuses for ignoring the call to financial freedom, because this extremely successful real estate investor and author will show you how to get started so you, too, can become a passive income physician.

Michael Becker
Principal, Strategic Properly Investment Advisory (SPI Advisory LLC)

# MONEY MEDICINE

He's disgruntled, often angry, and difficult to manage. He's uncooperative, easily offended, and at times, explodes at colleagues and curses out of frustration. There are some obvious reasons for his antisocial behavior: He works nights, weekends, and holidays, and the hours he puts in every month are excessive, especially given the stressful nature of his professional environment.

He might also be reacting to an unhappy marriage, or maybe he has already suffered through a divorce or two. This tends to make him brittle and defensive in relationships, including those he must endure with nurses and patients. He receives poor scores on satisfaction surveys because he just doesn't care anymore. His bedside manner has been swallowed up in all this stress, and he is about to lose his job, which will force him to seek employment elsewhere, possibly a greater distance from his current residence.

In spite of all this, the man I'm describing is not a bad person. He is a physician in his sixties, and long ago, the good doctor began his career with the best of intentions. He was young, idealistic, and dead set on saving the world and helping others.

Now, in the twilight of his career, he growls and dismisses the good will of his staff and peers because he is desperate. He knows his earning years are coming to an end, his physical and mental health are deteriorating, and he has not properly prepared for retirement. That's why he takes on a workload that would challenge the stamina of a younger man, because he is trying to compensate for the poor way he managed his money in the peak years of his professional life.

But it didn't have to be this way. See, Dr. Desperate has a long-lost colleague named Dr. Bliss. Both exhibit impressive IQs, have amazing aptitude for the sciences, and boast diplomas and degrees earned at top-rated schools. They even once shared the same office.

So why is Dr. Desperate working himself to death in the middle of the night while Dr. Bliss no longer has to keep long hours, preferring to sail his yacht on the high seas? The answer is rather simple: foresight.

Dr. Desperate never learned anything about investing. Instead, he handed his earnings over to a fee-based money manager and assumed everything would take care of itself. It didn't. His money didn't multiply at an acceptable rate, nor did he learn about the power of passive income. Since his net worth didn't expand much, he lived below his means. He trusted the myth too many of us are taught and naively believe: "Get a good education, invest in the stock market, choose a profession that provides security, and everything will be sunny skies, kid!"

Perhaps he was misled by a so-called financial guru, someone who made big promises that did more harm than good. Since the doc was a hands-off money guy, he did not notice or take command of the problem until it was too late to recover, and the two divorces with their costly attorneys and alimony didn't help much either. There is another possibility though. Perhaps he bought into the conventional wisdom that plagues so many physicians. Perhaps he believed the notion that he had to focus solely on his work in lieu of pursuing personal happiness and other interests that would refresh his body, mind, and spirit.

Meanwhile, while they were all still in their fabulous forties, the yacht doc and five other professionals sat down one day and decided to create equity in their own business. They no longer merely provided services; rather, they also invested in and owned real estate, the cornerstone that housed their wealth, which in turn, produced passive income. Like their paychecks, the money arrives monthly, but there is one big difference: Investment income is independent of how many hours they spend working clinically.

In short, Dr. Bliss and his colleagues began to invest in themselves and their own dreams rather than working a lifetime just to contribute to someone else's success. They paid themselves first and, in a sense, repaid themselves for the singular but relatively expensive commitment that was necessary to join the medical profession in the first place.

As a result, each yacht doctor grew an impressive net worth that eventually created enormous and passive wealth. In other words, they no longer had to work as doctors. They could stop chasing the proverbial paycheck that would supposedly provide a luxurious retirement. They were financially able to retire at any point and only worked clinically when they wanted. They still enjoyed being physicians but only on their own terms. No longer slaves to administrators and bureaucrats, they could finally practice the real art of medicine, finally pursue their passion instead of just plowing through for pay.

Dr. Bliss's way of life has only one lamentable downside: He now must listen to his colleague, Dr. Desperate, complain that he too should have expanded his horizons. The truth is, the opportunity came knocking more than once, but Dr. Desperate, desperate as he was, turned it away every time.

My tale of two doctors begs one important question: Are you headed for desperation or bliss?

Dr. Desperate's predicament is frightening but preventable. Dr. Bliss's carefree life does not come without discipline and desire, but it is achievable, even for those physicians who are the first to admit that they lack common sense in money matters. In the following pages, I reveal how a lackluster high school student with no hope for college joined the United States Navy, excelled, then stumbled badly, served overseas in our Middle East conflict, and finally redeemed himself by answering the call to become a doctor. That's not where my story ends though.

During my residency, I developed an interest in real estate, bought my first property, and finally realized I had a passion that went far beyond my zeal for medicine. What was that passion?

Simple: I wanted the freedom to spend my days on this good Earth in any way that I wished. Why would I want to wait for retirement? I wanted the kind of wealth that would guarantee I would never become Dr. Desperate. This was not an idle decision for me, and it will not be for anyone else either. I, too, have spent many years administering to patients in various Emergency Department settings. I know the terrain and the character traits that define us all. I know many Dr. Desperates but few Dr. Blisses.

As physicians and surgeons, we dedicate ourselves to saving and improving the lives of others. However, the demands placed on us being on call twenty-four hours a day, working nights, holidays and odd hours can erode our health and happiness. Sleep and circadian rhythm disorders reduce life expectancy, and we have a higher likelihood of high blood pressure and diabetes.

Sadly, as we grow older, if shaky finances demand that we push ourselves to work even longer hours, we become vulnerable to four common stages of descent:

- We disconnect and don't develop supportive relationships.

- Chronic depression sets in.

- Substance abuse often ensues.

- Suicide is considered and often carried out.

You may wonder if a dedicated professional who has taken the Hippocratic Oath can really be tempted to take his or her own life, and the sad answer is a resounding yes. I personally know of five such tragedies taking place in just a ten-year span. As sad as this is, tragic consequences are not restricted to emergency doctors; other types of physicians, dentists, and therapists often face desperate times.

Why join me though? What can I possibly teach you?

For starters, I am a former full-time physician who now manages a network of hospitals. My real estate investing has allowed me to translate my high income into a high net worth, the measure of wealth that assures stability now and in the twilight years of life.

Although there are many types of passive income, the purpose of this book is not to define every path for recurring revenue on investments.

Instead, I will guide you through the basic concept of making money outside your profession, in the hopes that you will see the light and change your ways while there is still time. My method for profoundly improving my own net worth continues to be multifamily and commercial real estate. Therefore, I rely on those experiences to show you how and why we must move beyond stocks and bonds to create lasting returns on our investments.

In spite of what you may hear, the decision to create passive income through various means and expand your net worth is not vain, arrogant, or a distraction from being an excellent healthcare professional. In fact, I have good reason to believe that having interests outside your practice is a tonic that may extend and improve your life while improving your financial stability.

It is time to take another kind of oath. Call it the Passive Income Promise, a vow that we will do everything in our power to always be profitable, pay ourselves first, and expand financial horizons while providing for the people we love in a dynamic, generous manner.

—Thomas Black, MD

# ONE

# CRITICAL FAILURE

My first passion in life was the great American pastime, baseball. I loved the sport, dreamed big baseball dreams, and enjoyed the camaraderie on the field with my friends. We were in awe of the athletes who could make the great catch or hit the game-saving home run.

I was not, however, a student-athlete, in that the hours I devoted to the game were not matched by productive study time. Far more interesting to me than all those boring notes and worksheets was my baseball card collection, which I'd subsidized with the meager fortune I'd earned renting my video games out to friends and cutting neighborhood lawns. If I'd had any business foresight, I might have hoarded and preserved those trading cards until they became valuable collector's items, twenty years hence.

I'm not losing sleep over having enjoyed a boy's

life though. We have to grab the fun in life while we can. Still, who among us doesn't look back on adolescence and occasionally cringe? If only I'd applied myself! If only I'd started saving earlier! If only …

I paid a price for my indifference toward academics and my acceptance of mediocrity. As high school came to a close, my choices were extremely limited. My SAT scores were such a disaster that there was no hope that any state university would welcome me, maybe not even a community college. Perhaps I was a candidate or at least a target audience member for the for-profit campuses that had sprung up. Fortunately, I had no money to throw at those ventures. At 17, I was on the road to ruin. Or was I?

Actually, the opportunities I did seize became seminal experiences, stepping stones. In those days, nobody—certainly not my parents—could have guessed that I would one day establish a career in medicine and discover a zeal for real estate that would lead to development projects and investments that have significantly expanded my net worth. Net worth? Back then, I'd never heard the term; even if I had, at that time, my assets amounted to my baseball mitt, cleats, and a shoebox full of collectibles.

Fortunately, my early stumbles and humbling misdeeds were not the end of the road. My future wasn't dead on arrival. The naïve and sometimes stupid mistakes I made were actually the wake-up calls I apparently needed to recognize the skills I possessed but had not embraced.

Were the setbacks frustrating? Absolutely. When it was obvious that higher education was not going to be an immediately available option, I focused on becoming a volunteer for the local Fire Department in Fort Worth, Texas. I applied myself and found the study materials engrossing. I attended every meeting they offered to prepare volunteer firefighters for the demanding profession, and I earned my CPR certification without a glitch. I thought I had found my calling.

**The naïve and sometimes stupid mistakes I made were actually the wake-up calls I apparently needed to recognize the skills I possessed but had not embraced.**

Hold your horses, rookie. Despite my dedication and desire, the application process did not work in my favor. I looked very young for my age, and it soon became apparent that I did not fit the model for future Fort Worth Firefighter of the Year. My excitement and commitment were snuffed out entirely when I was notified that there was no position available for me. It felt as though I'd been fired, and at first, I felt hollow and dejected.

Perhaps you are familiar with this old adage, "When the going gets tough, the tough get going." I can't say I was tough back then; desperate was more like it. What choice did I have but to get up, brush myself off, and find another window of opportunity? My friends were busy thinking about the freshman year at college, or some had plans to attend vocational schools or join their family business, maybe even travel for a year before returning to the great halls of learning. What about me though? What would I do with myself?

The day the Fire Department turned me down, the family phone rang. When I answered it, a Navy recruiter led me to believe that the military service had all sorts of exciting advantages to offer: training in critical areas like technology and more, global sailing on the open seas, and national pride. At first, I balked at the idea.

My father, a middleclass family man with a management position in a large corporation, had served in the United States Air Force and had often pestered me about looking into the armed forces. Traditionally, the choice was a way to dig out of the academic hole some young men dig for themselves, gain some worldly experience, and, in general, grow up. Despite parental urgings and the positive sales pitch of the Navy recruiter, though, I just couldn't see myself in that role. The military? No way!

I was only 17, though, so Dad's firm suggestion prevailed. I was sternly instructed to "At least go down to the recruiting office, keep an open mind, and learn more about the opportunities."

Or, I could always flip hamburgers for minimum wage, donning a cheap polo shirt and a baseball cap with the company logo. When my college friends came home on the holidays, I would be there to take their orders: *"Hey, Franky, do you want extra cheese on that double-bacon burger...and you want me to supersize your fries?"*

How do you spell d-e-a-d e-n-d, and is it served on a sesame seed bun?

Reluctantly, I trudged to my appointment and was greeted by clean-cut men in neatly pressed uniforms. They were welcoming, enthusiastic, and filled with life purpose that went far beyond what the drive-thru window would ever offer. They painted pictures of glory and personal satisfaction. In hushed tones, they convinced me that I was needed and that I could and should make a valuable contribution to our nation, the United States of America.

I agreed to take an aptitude exam and undergo an extensive physical. To my surprise, I scored well on the test, so I was granted my choice of job paths. Dang, life sure was looking up, courtesy of a little boost of self-confidence from Uncle Sam.

This has probably happened to you once or twice. Convinced you would prefer to zig rather than zag, turn left not right, or wear red and not blue, you are handed the opposite. Nevertheless, in spite of the U-turn, you thrive.

Soon after my meeting with recruiters, I arrived

at boot camp, survived that ordeal, and was sent to the Great Lakes Naval Training Center near Chicago. There, something clicked. The indifferent kid who had earned lousy grades in high school suddenly began to apply himself. The topic was fascinating, and I had a facility and capacity for learning, something I never realized about myself while I was in the throes of surviving public schools. The Navy taught me a trade and helped me develop the skills needed to maintain and repair radar and satellite communications systems, real sophisticated stuff and a far cry from fast food. *"Yo, Tommy, you work the deep fryer today!"*

Anchors aweigh. I graduated first in my electronics class and earned a chance to attend Naval Academy prep school, a one-year intensive that was basically a remedial program that would fill in the blanks left over from my not-so-great performance in high school. Equally encouraging was being awarded a Broaden Opportunity Officer Selection in Training (BOOST) fellowship. These rewards meant that after I completed the coursework, I would earn a full scholarship to any college that offered a Naval Recruit Office Training (ROTC) program. That was quite a leap for a guy who, in the previous year, was essentially locked out of higher education due to poor grades. My turnaround would be a key reminder in later years that even our darkest hours can be quickly redeemed with focused effort. Striving for excellence is a decision. As a boy,

I invested a lot of hard work and time in honing my baseball skills and building my card collection. In that environment, I was inspired by watching superstar athletes dazzle on televised Major League games, yet that same drive did not translate to other areas of my life.

That changed after I performed so well in my electronics classes and gained respect from my peers and instructors. Attainment is the match that lights the candle. Sometimes it comes as a surprise, but the impact is the same. My new status launched some lofty goals that would have been unthinkable when I was 17. Now they actually seemed within reach.

> Despite the initial pain, this established an essential belief, a life lesson: Never, ever give up.

I would become a naval officer and study to become a fighter pilot. The skills I gleaned would allow me take off from and land on an aircraft carrier floating in the middle of the ocean. I trembled with passion as I imagined all that I would accomplish and how quickly I would accomplish it, if only I could stay out of trouble. That, my friends, turned out to be a big if.

Youth is a virus, one its young carriers do not even know is lurking deep within. Sometimes it is benign and does no harm. Some grow out of it, eventually and at their own pace. Unfortunately, there are also moments when it cannot help but betray, seemingly attacking its host out of nowhere.

My Naval Academy appointment was not meant to be. Instead, I would take a hard fall that would tarnish my reputation and status, humiliate me among my peers, and put a blunt stop to what I hoped would be a swift ascent. The beat-down would force me to start over again and begrudgingly retrace my steps from the bottom of the heap.

Despite the initial pain, it established an essential belief: Never give up.

## Passive Income Physician takeaways!

- Perseverance is the gift we receive after hitting rock bottom.

- Failure in the moment does not portend failure forever. Failure is pivotal in the learning process.

- Opportunity arrives when least expected.

- New possibilities—destiny, maybe—may take us in wonderful directions we might not ever have considered.

## TWO

# A ZEAL FOR EXCELLENCE

This will shock you: Young men like to have fun. Even more important, they like to fit in with the crowd they run with.

I left home at 17 to join the Navy. To my utter amazement, I quickly found my stride, excelled in my studies, and was surrounded by a bunch of guys who liked and befriended me and invited me to hang out.

To be sure, I was thrilled to join them. We enjoyed all food, jokes, pranks, encouragement, and so many other forms of camaraderie that come with shared experience. We could be loud and competitive, of course, because we were proud, determined Navy men on a path that would take most of us around the world and some to great heights we never thought possible for our futures.

The months passed, and time eventually ushered in milestones of note, such as my eighteenth and nineteenth birthdays. These were not mere numbers to me. I enjoyed my time with my new crew, but it should also be said that most of them were several years older, 22, 23, and so on. I was eager to catch up, but it wasn't because the extra years made them smarter than me or better sailors. Their birthdates distinguished them in one and only one way: They could saunter into a bar and legally drink.

When your friends are ordering rounds of beer and shots of whiskey, you prefer to join in; there is something humiliating about having to whisper, "Uh…I guess I'll have a Coke." Such a murmuring made a ribbing from my tribe a sure thing. It was all good-natured, just the banter of a boys' night out, but after a while, it was completely unacceptable to me.

Some guys were big and brawny, so bouncers and barkeeps never suspected that they were underage. This was not the case for me. My looks were decidedly boyish and would remain so even after I passed the magical and arbitrary threshold of 21—not to mention that it was my first time away from home. Out on my own, free of the nest, I wanted to spread my wings.

One day, I decided that it was pointless to run with the wolves if I couldn't also share a couple drinks after class. The solution, it seemed to me, was obvious.

The first time I was carded at a bar and showed my new fake ID, I was nervous. The credential looked real enough, even if I still appeared to be about 12 years old. Once I got in the habit of flashing it before I was even asked, it became second nature, no big deal. By then, I'd accomplished a great deal and was feeling quite capable and—dare I say it—even worldly.

That all came to an end in the final week of my training. By then, I'd been named class president and was in charge of about 100 recruits. I'd also been notified that I'd been selected for the educational fellowships I mentioned earlier. Everything I did throughout my school day was to further me in my honorable quest to become a naval officer. My sights were set on Annapolis and pilot training as we anticipated our transition to our fleet assignments, and I would be heading for a vessel docked in Japan. Then, disaster struck.

As class president, I was responsible for organizing my men. We formed up outside and marched, military style. The drill was all about leadership, discipline, and teamwork. One day, I rushed out to the field to perform our maneuvers and inadvertently left my backpack in a hallway in the training facility. I was told that officials who searched its contents were only trying to determine who owned it, a process that took hours, far longer than it should have. After locating my wallet, which certainly should have cleared up the identity mystery, they rooted deeper, only to discover my false identification. Just like that, I had met my Waterloo. No big deal, right? Just typical nonsense from a young man who had not yet turned 20 and was away from home for the first time? Tell that to the U.S. Navy. To make matters worse, the day I was dressed down by my superiors, I received a letter announcing my appointment to the U.S. Naval Academy.

The repercussions were seismic, in part because before I won the appointment for officer training, that enviable honor, I'd interviewed with admirals. Obviously, I'd made an impression. In the opinion of those decorated, high-ranking men, I was a person of character and intelligence, a young man who might one day lead a fleet of ships or pilot a jet fighter or—wash dishes in the officers' mess hall.

They busted me, big time. After leading the way for so many of my peers, I was demoted two ranks below every other graduate. I lost everything, including my assignment in Japan and any hope of becoming an aviator.

My poor decision to fake my age meant I'd also squandered the many hours I'd volunteered and drilled with other cadets. I might as well have collected all that effort into a heap, drenched it in alcohol, and set it on fire. My dreams were gone, up in smoke, and I was toast.

The next stop for me was a guided-missile destroyer afloat somewhere in the Pacific. My first job was to clean toilets and mop floors. It was grueling but was at least good, honest work. I had endless hours to reflect on my fall from grace.

As a child growing up in a middleclass family in the heartland, my father was born into poverty, but he raised himself up and enjoyed a decent career. From those experiences came the common advice of the times, bland exhortations to work hard, without much context that expanded the vision of life beyond mere labor and a humble paycheck. Was it too much to ask that the sons and daughters of middleclass people might become wealthy?

Brooding while making the Navy urinals sparkle, I realized that my schooling was unremarkable mostly because I'd grown accustomed to my own mediocrity. I was happy with it and knew how to function within those bleak parameters. The Navy, though, had awakened something in me that was astonishing: ambition. Through my Navy training, I discovered that I had far more to offer than I ever suspected and that I enjoyed applying myself and taking on challenges.

> From those experiences came the common advice of the times—bland exhortations to work hard without much context that expanded the vision of life beyond mere labor a humble paycheck .

Those thoughts, marinating in the scent of human waste and disinfectant, were what kept me moving forward.

Still, there was no quick turnaround in my status. The pain would not stop.

Soon, I was placed in the officers' quarters. For three months I would assist the group of officers whose ranks I had hoped to join. The proximity to my former yearnings was excruciating, like a cruel joke, with me being the punchline. Ironing their uniforms daily and serving breakfast to them every morning did serve an important purpose though: Those tasks ignited a new fire in me.

The following three years saw me deployed to the Persian Gulf, twice. Following those assignments, I joined a counter-narcotics operation in South America. While serving, I enrolled in every correspondence course available to sailors at sea, and my mind roiled like the raging sea, full of new ideas and possibilities. Throughout the ordeal, my mother was always encouraging. Father, however, was a different story. To this day, I can vividly recall the time I called home with important news. I was about 23 then, and I had seen a bit of the world, had painted new vistas and bigger mountaintops that I wanted to scale. While dialing their number, I could barely contain my excitement. "Dad, I've decided to become a doctor."

He laughed.

At the time, my feelings were bruised. In hindsight, I know Dad could not possibly have been aware of the transformation I was undergoing. Through no fault of his own, he could not grasp what burned in me, the horizons I'd discovered that stretched far beyond the containment of my Midwestern upbringing. I now realize that such a dismaying response is what many of us experience when we share new goals, especially those that seem uncharacteristic. Even the best of friends might be confused or groan when they hear for the first time about an interest in a career change or a new passion for travel or even real estate. How easy it is for others to be critical or simply not intuit the combustive need we feel to expand the realm of possibilities.

> ...his boy who had shown a common taste for mediocrity had grown into a man who now had the confidence and zeal to excel.

To his credit, years later, Dad admitted as much. His boy, who had shown a common taste for mediocrity, had grown into a man who now had the confidence and zeal to excel.

It should also be said that Dad was not the only skeptic. After all, wasn't I the numbskull who had betrayed his own ascent with a stupid stunt, messing up my life for the sake of a few shots? Wasn't I the kid who was demoted to the lower depths of military service, forced to clean toilets? Now this stumblebum wants to be a doctor? Preposterous.

I agree. It *was* preposterous, yet it all came true.

## Passive Income Physician takeaways!

- Humility frees us from the shackles of disappointment.

- Opposition helps to shape courage and actionable strategies.

- Naysayers are insects that may annoy but not foil commitment to greatness.

## THREE

# REJECTING INEXPERIENCE

My deployments to the Persian Gulf gave me the opportunity to broaden my education with a variety of correspondence courses, but the learning did not end there. Since my rank was lower than that of my colleagues, rather than working in my field of electronics, I was expected to fulfill many of the basic duties that have to happen daily on board a large vessel.

Maintenance was a never-ending chore because we were at war with salt water, an erosive, toxic enemy that never sleeps. As a result, I found myself constantly grinding decks, welding railings, and painting and repainting surfaces. While some of the tasks were mind-numbingly boring, others were extremely challenging simply because I'd never done them before. I was forced to take the initiative and figure things out for myself, on the spot.

It became a revelatory experience. Hands-on experience and a multitude of mistakes were brutal teachers at times, yet they also became my most prized lessons. Some say military service will toughen a young person up. In my experience, it *opened* me up. I was shoved into a vast, previously unexplored territory of my capabilities. I was stunned that I could move past my inexperience so quickly to achieve such meaningful results.

> I was forced to take the initiative and figure things out for myself, on the spot.

Think about this for a moment: We put our eyes on a prize that glitters with so much promise. Then, through immaturity or fate, we lose our way and are forced into a type of circumstance that seems subpar or degrading. Next, we make profound discoveries about our personal resourcefulness and depth of character. In time, we emerge as better, better-rounded people.

How is this possible? Was I wrong to covet an appointment to the Naval Academy, to hunger for a place among the ranks of officers? Of course not. To this day, though, I occasionally wonder: *What if…?*

I would not trade my learning path for the gold brocade of an admiral's uniform. Laboring on the decks of Navy vessels in the Middle East, doing grunt work that was harsh and without glory, I became a man who was better prepared to face my future. Over

18

time, I realized that rank, in and of itself, does not fully measure a human being. Even years later, when I became an emergency room physician, a position of superiority in the minds of many average citizens, it was not the medical degree that gave me the courage to try new things. I did not think, *Hey, I'm a doctor now. I'm smart, so I'll do well when I invest in real estate.*

**Hands on experience and a multitude of mistakes could be brutal teachers, and yet they also became my most prized.**

There is one reason I now am avidly engaged in growing my net worth with passive income from multifamily and commercial properties. As a demoted sailor on a U.S. Navy destroyer, knocked about by disappointment, I developed one crucial belief: Inexperience cannot stop me—never, ever.

From that point on, I took massive action whenever I was ready to achieve new, seemingly impossible goals. Dreams are inert, a dime a dozen, without decisive actions.

As I said in the previous chapter, others will scoff when you set your sails to carry you toward something entirely new. The negativity may surprise you, but the jeers may actually be a good sign.

Justin Turner was an unwanted utility player for the New York Mets when he was traded to the

Los Angeles Dodgers on a Minor League contract. Unhappy with his role, he decided to change his approach to the game. He was known for base hits, nothing showy. Now, he wanted to become a slugger and work his way back into a Major League lineup. Thus, the third baseman took massive action in three profound ways:

- He changed his diet to reshape his physique. He consulted a sports psychologist.

- He hired a hitting coach to work with him in the off-season to retool his swing.

Turner's transformation was not immediate, but he knew his fortune had changed when he hit six home runs in a row during batting practice at spring training. No, it wasn't the flight of the ball that surprised him; it was the flak he took from other players. They chided him for swinging for the fences: "That's not who you are."Exactly. The ball player was tired of his former self, because it was holding him back. The criticism from others annoyed Turner, but he didn't protest or bother to explain. Instead, he used it to fuel the fire in his belly. Three years later, he was an elite power hitter in the Major League Baseball. His value to the team had increased to the tune of a four-year sixty-four million dollar contract inked in 2017.

Some doctors might not be impressed with

Turner's story. After all, surviving medical school is a major feat in its own right, an all-consuming task that demands numerous adjustments. By improving his skills, the ball player may have stepped out of his comfort zone but not into an entirely new profession such as real estate.

Fair enough; however, the story does shine light on a man who was willing to break free of old habits and the expectations of others to make a better life for himself. Now, let's broaden the story and define Turner's athletic skills as an asset that was not fully utilized. Thanks to the effort he made to retool the asset, his new contract will undoubtedly pay him many millions of dollars—not the kind of money a Minor League player in a rut could expect.

The asset I want physicians to focus on is annual income. How is the money game working out? Do your investments prove that all the hard work you poured into becoming a medical professional was worth it? Or do you feel like you're still in the minor leagues financially, struggling to pay down student loans and a home mortgage while raising children and saving for their education? One more question: Are you willing to take action and retool your annual income to ensure better results?

When I bought a foreclosed, three-acre lot for $30,000 to build my first multifamily apartment complex, I took a lot of grief from family, friends, and colleagues in the medical profession. They thought I was nuts and did not mind telling me so.

Perhaps their doubts about my decision rattled me a bit, because on the day I arrived at the lending institution to finalize the deal, I paused before putting my signature on the contract. The banker noticed my apprehension and knew I was inexperienced. He chuckled and said, "Son, you may not make as much money as you expect, but you're going to make money."

He was right. On that day, I became a *player*.

It had nothing to do with earning my medical credentials though. Rather, my first development project led to more real estate success because I trusted the lesson I'd learned while busting my hump in the open sea, saving a U.S. Navy destroyer from salt water assaults.

---

### *Passive Income Physician* takeaways!

- Inexperience is no excuse for ignoring opportunity.

- Massive action converts dream into reality.

---

FOUR

# Flawed Thinking

Five years of military service elapsed before my college education formally began at the University of North Texas (UNT). I was excited because, in my view, my education at sea was the perfect preamble for this next stage of growth. I was more mature than most of my classmates, I was very ambitious, and I had honed skills that would help me reach my goals. In fact, I was already within reach of my first college degree.

I'd completed so many correspondence courses from Central Texas College (CTC) in Killeen while deployed in the Navy that I was very close to earning my associates degree in business applications. To complete the requirements, I enrolled in a couple appropriate classes at UNT, transferred those credits to CTC, and was awarded a diploma, all while carrying a double-major in biology and biochemistry. I did well and finished in three years near the top of my class. Fortunately, throughout my university years, I was on full scholarship, so I could concentrate on my studies and the volunteering that was part of the curriculum.

I also took a job with Wells Fargo as a credit analysist. By then, I had expanded my financial vocabulary through voracious reading, and I intuitively understood salesmanship and how to communicate with people. This was in the late 1990s, when the market was heating up and homeowners were inclined to live large and take equity out of their property. The fun would end, of course, when the mortgage crisis hit in 2008.

> That same flawed thinking that limits most homeowners from developing wealth through thoughtful multifamily property acquisition.

Nevertheless, my love of money and how it works was evident, even though I had not yet discovered the power and leverage of real estate. While cold calling, I was enthralled with the idea of buying a home and then selling it at some future date for a profit.

That same flawed thinking limits most homeowners from developing wealth through thoughtful multifamily property acquisition. I had other reasons for waiting to buy a home though. While at UNT, I'd met a young woman named Micaela, a smart and ambitious person. We dated for about a year before I asked her to marry me. I was five years older and ready to have a regular, settled life after so many years at sea. I knew she was the one for me, and I told her so. We planned to wed in July, after her May graduation. By the time I reached Galveston for a four-year stint (2002-06) at the University of Texas Medical Branch, Micaela was teaching entrepreneurship in a local high school, and I was much too busy for anything but medicine. As newlyweds, we were tempted to tiptoe into the scary waters of home ownership, and we actually found a small house we liked and put money down on it, an investment we lost when we backed out. The property was in a municipal utilities district, which meant a higher tax rate; after diving in, we feared we would struggle to pay the bill.

That incident was the hallmark of the narrow-minded thinking I'd learned growing up. Do the math: Either you can afford it or you can't. No one in my circle encouraged me to take a leap and learn. It just wasn't done.

My father, for example, reminded me that I didn't have a real income, that I was a med student who'd only be in Galveston for four years. In hindsight, those were *not* insurmountable hurdles. I could have used my Veterans' Administration home loan to get us in, and Micaela and I would have somehow held on and probably made some money on the deal. Compare that simple, single-family deal with the complex I purchased recently for thirteen million dollars. Did I have that amount of money lying around? Of course not. Who does? Creative financing allowed me to make the investment.

As for quashing the purchase of a house because you don't intend to spend the rest of your life in the community, remember that we live in a mobile society. Micaela and I could have rented the home out after my schooling in Galveston and used those fees to pay down the mortgage. There is no magic formula, no crystal ball that will tell you when to buy real estate and when not to.

> **Fear is an insidious thief. It robs us of our best intentions, ideas, and the opportunities that will help us grow and create wealth.**

I regretted being talked out of my first real estate deal. Whenever I drove through that neighborhood, I gritted my teeth and shook my head because I knew the value of those small homes had increased.

Fear is an insidious thief. It robs us of our best intentions, ideas, and the opportunities that will help us grow and create wealth. Fear defeats us at every turn if we allow it to, because there will always be something that makes us shudder or sweat. It holds us back from greatness.

Eventually, I discovered that if you have clear goals, a little fear and stress can serve as great motivators. Of course I don't advocate getting in over your head and defaulting on loans, but freedom with passive income is possible once investors learn how to use debt to their advantage.

But guess what? Flawed thinking is not restricted to guys like me, people who grew up middleclass. Although I did not have time to flourish as a real estate investor while in medical school, through osmosis, I was expanding my financial education. Where? In the operating room, of all places.

It was fascinating to listen to the mature, attending physicians talk about their stock market investments as we prepared for surgery. One doctor had a hot tip, and another complained about his listless hedge fund. An anesthesiologist could often be found reading the *Wall Street Journal* while waiting for the medical procedure to commence.

These mentors were people of intelligence and stature who taught me a great deal about medicine. I'll always be grateful for their guidance in that, but little did I know they were also giving me an even greater gift by revealing how *not* to invest.

These days, I take calls from experienced doctors who just can't get ahead with their retirement money, despite constantly calling their stockbrokers and mutual fund managers. Their thinking in financial matters is flawed because their medical education was intense and their full attention and commitment, leaving them no time to really delve into and learn about another topic. This is why so many physicians end up relying on so-called market experts to sell them conventional financial instruments, primarily paper assets in a 401(k) environment. In the beginning, that was all I knew too.

> They are flawed in their thinking about financial matters because their medical education was intense and demanded their full attention and commitment.

My awakening was gradual and coincided with the impact of enormous changes in the medical field. Doctors were facing declining medical insurance reimbursements and increased red tape. Patients were dissatisfied and, in some cases, angry, demanding perfect medicinal and surgical outcomes while taking no responsibility whatsoever for their own health. Even physicians who operated successful private practices and employed many staff members found it difficult to stay afloat.

Enter the huge corporate entities with a solution: We'll take over your practice and make you our employee. We'll pay you a decent base salary to do what you do best, to be a doctor, and you'll also be granted a generous amount of paid vacation time annually. Best of all, you'll never again have to deal with complicated, time-consuming paperwork, and we'll take care of any and all malpractice claims.

I can't blame doctors for warming to such an offer. Large companies have more power and money to negotiate with hospitals and insurance companies, and smaller, democratically run private groups cannot compete. For the same reasons, smaller hospital systems consolidate with big national entities. If you can't fight them, you may feel like you have to join them. As a result, many doctors gave up their 1099 status to become W-2 employees. They no longer had to think like business owners, but in that, they also surrendered the freedom to build their practice so they could expand revenue and assets. Like it or not, the Affordable Care Act (ACA) played a role in this transformation. If our nation's healthcare plan eventually evolves into a single-payer (government-controlled) system, physicians will be the employees of a government that operates with a multitrillion-dollar deficit. Do we want our senators and representatives setting our annual salaries when they spend so much time debating our nation's budget?

Again, there are some benefits to accepting an employer-employee relationship, but these pros must be measured against the cons of the financial limitations inherent in the deal: namely, retirement funds.

For example, if you work in the trenches for twenty years for a corporate group that pays an annual salary of $400,000 with a 401(k) match at 4 percent, even if you max out your fund, you will not have anywhere near what you need to retire comfortably. How can this be? Let's say $50,000 per year is invested in your 401(k) for two decades, for a total of $1,000,000. This sounds good, right? Americans love the idea of a million bucks, the label of a millionaire, but can it stand up to inflation and other economic upheavals?

The scenario may make a lot of sense for the millennial generation that famously looks askance at home ownership, largely due to the economy and inflated home values, in favor of renting and enjoying a high-end lifestyle. There is nothing wrong with this, but we can't afford to be fooled by Wall Street, consumerism, and a soaring stock market. Change is inevitable. We cannot naïvely assume that over the course of a twenty- or thirty-year career, there will be no unexpected bumps in the road to retirement. Regardless, physicians who are willing to broaden their view of how money multiplies should be excited. Why? Because there is so much more potential for their impressive earning power. My mind was blown wide open after I finished medical school and headed to Indianapolis, Indiana for my residency. There, I befriended a man I initially assumed to be a bit mad and irresponsible, simply because he didn't have a

401(k) or IRA; his seemingly insane retirement plan was real estate investing. "These homes I've purchased and rent to families are my retirement," he said. *What?* I thought.

Then he patiently explained the strategy and numbers, giving me a peek at his income streams. This set off another barrage of voracious reading and inspired Micaela and me to finally buy our first house. We bought it on the bubble of the mortgage crisis, but in the end, it didn't matter. We were in the game.

### *Passive Income Physician* takeaways!

- Go ahead and crunch the numbers, but before you utter, "I can't," get creative.

- A steady salary is a benefit only if it is put to good, expansive use.

- Live like a millennial but think like an entrepreneur.

FIVE

# FIRST HOUSE

In 2006, we moved to Indianapolis, and I underwent training in the Indiana University Emergency Medicine Residency Program. It was intense. By then, Micaela and I had two very young children, but I saw very little of them in those three years. Instead, I spent over 100 hours a week in the hospital doing rotations and learning the art of my craft, all the while yearning for a different life. Laughable, right? Why would I put all that effort into medicine when I wanted something else? The truth is, most doctors in training experience escapist fantasies.

Before we made the move north from Texas, Micaela and I were determined to buy our first home. To get some help I began cold calling real estate agents in Indianapolis. We preferred a small boutique firm that would guide us in a friendly, hands-on manner.

Eventually, I met a realtor I'll call TR. We talked, and I liked his approach and decided to team up with him.

When Micaela and I bought our home, we had no inkling that a mortgage crisis was looming. We were just like all the other young couples who had accepted the generational wisdom that owning a house was essential, a major event, possibly the biggest investment of our lifetimes. Then, when the bubble burst, there was panic in the streets, including on Wall Street.

At the time, that bursting bubble didn't mean a whole lot to me. Yes, we had paid a premium for the property, and the value would drop significantly during the tumult of good money gone bad; however, we were still able to make our monthly mortgage payment, and we needed a place to live.

When it was time to sell, I was awakened to the nightmare experienced by so many others. *Where are the buyers?* I wondered, only to discover that they were scared away by the mortgage market collapse. Either that, or they were first-time buyers who no longer qualified for loans. After practically giving away funds and fanning the flames of an inflated real estate market, the banks revised their policies. Money was tight.

That was when naïfs like me realized that all the jabber about fulfilling the American Dream by owning a home was an empty promise. A home is not necessarily a reliable asset; appreciation of value is not guaranteed. Some homeowners realized that their homes were liabilities, and they were forced into fore-closure. Others sold at a loss. Why? Because they had to relocate for new jobs, were going through divorces, or they were facing other life-altering dilemmas and traumas. Disappointment invaded the Promised Land, and that American Dream was now a nightmare, seem-ingly inescapable.

> **A home is not necessarily a reliable asset; appreciation of value is not guaranteed.**

Although my medical studies left me very lit-tle time to read more about real estate and Micaela had her hands full raising our children, TR and I had become friends and talked a lot. He explained that realtors were independent contractors, not employ-ees. The firm he was associated with did not offer a pension plan, so it was his responsibility to invest in his future. To heck with stocks and bonds, the paper assets preferred by the physicians who mentored me. TR chose what he knew best: real estate.

Cash flow and leverage became key topics in my discussions with the brilliant man, and I squeezed in some reading to expand my grasp of these concepts. TR opened my mind with simple examples such as buying a home with a monthly mortgage payment of $400 and renting it out for $1,200, to produce a stream of income. Those who had multiple homes with a positive cash flow after taxes and maintenance could enjoy something most people know nothing about: passive income—that is, money that arrives every month without you having to work overtime. Passive income is precisely what it says: It grows your wealth passively, all because you took a risk and invested wisely.

In light of the banking crisis, Micaela and I weighed our options. We could sell at a loss and move wherever my first job took us or I could look for a job in the area and hope for a positive uptick in the economy.

TR, of course, encouraged us to follow his path: "The market will improve. Be patient. In the meantime, why not rent your home out to someone who is just beginning his or her residency? You know they will be here for at least a few years, and I'll manage the place for you if you move out of state."

When TR and I first met, he had never worked with residents coming to town to complete their medical training, but as he taught me about real estate, I shared what I knew about the many residency programs. It soon became his specialty, his niche. Renting my first house to a newbie in town was a perfect fit, and it was a big relief when we decided to take a staff position in east Texas.

Here's the lowdown: For three years, another doctor-to-be paid down our mortgage while living in a home that slowly regained value. When that physician was ready to leave the area in 2012, Micaela and I sold our first house for a profit.

Not bad for rookies, huh? Of course I can't take much credit, because we had an excellent teacher. TR helped us escape the flawed thinking that got us into home ownership, and he articulated some basic truths that debunked misleading ideas. One of these was: "You don't get rich selling real estate. You get rich *owning* real estate."

> "You don't get rich selling real estate. You get rich owning real estate."

Many first-time investors dream of a windfall, holding on to property often provides amazing dividends, otherwise known as passive income. Therefore, when working with buyers, TR often preaches the benefits of acquisition. "I know this home is a nice place to live," he says, "but when you're ready to move, you might want to hold on to this one in an investment portfolio." Why? Taxation." For example, the young physicians TR now works with obviously have the potential to make generous annual incomes, but the higher the income, the harder it becomes to find deductions. Owning property is a legitimate method of reducing taxes. On paper, it may appear that the investor is suffering a loss, after subtracting monthly expenses from rent; however, in the big picture, the renter pays for the mortgage (passive income) while the owner claims depreciation of the property on his taxes. It's a lose-win situation that is completely legal.

But what happens to a portfolio of real estate during market turmoil, such as the 2008 collapse? Even if you, the investor, have to negotiate a lower monthly rental fee to avoid vacancies, it will affect cash flow without crushing you, as long as your business has been well managed. Compare that scenario to the stock market meltdown in the late 1990s, when some high-flying internet companies—paper assets for investors—went from ridiculously inflated valuations to zero.

**Property will always be worth something because it doesn't suddenly disappear.**

Property will always be worth something because it doesn't suddenly disappear.

Granted, in the early going, after buying a couple properties, the numbers may not be impressive. Perhaps only a small amount of capital is available for down payments, so the property does not yet exhibit much equity. All the while, though, the investor learns much from the process of acquisition. One lesson in particular is the power of leverage.

When interest rates are low, money is cheap. In this environment, experienced investors like TR may borrow as much as possible, knowing that, say, a 3 percent lending rate is easily paid back if the property is paying 7 percent each month. If the lending rate is 6 percent, would that same property still look good to the investor? Maybe not. Now, money is tighter, and this might make for a stingy cash flow. In a previous chapter, I confessed that my first impulses to buy property were quashed by the mantra of flawed thinking: *I can't afford it.* Then I revealed that in recent years, I purchased a multifamily property valued at about thirteen million. What changed in me? I finally came to understand and trust how a relatively small amount of money can provide the rights and benefits of ownership. That's leverage. Also, by the way, by improving operations (lowering expenses) and increasing revenue (raising rent), in nine months, that $12.8 million property grew to a $16.9 million value.

Multifamily is clearly my chosen path to early retirement. In the forthcoming chapters, I'll share much about the exponential advantages of investing in this type of property, as well as my discovery that commercial sites, such as light industrial and storage facilities, offer many of the same benefits.

First, though, before we leave the single-family home arena, let's use a typical scenario to suggest how this business model can provide a retirement. Eventually, renters have paid off the mortgage, leaving the owner free and clear of debt. That means every monthly rent check represents positive cash flow and abundant passive income.

Investors are wise to target a level of monthly income that will provide an ample retirement. Is that $10,000 monthly or much more? In any case, how fast you meet that requirement will depend on how many properties you purchase and how quickly the mortgages are paid down. Of course there is a catch or two. When Micaela and I decided to rent our home in Indianapolis, we had the option to leave it in the hands of TR, who kindly managed the property for three years. If not for that friendship, we would have had to hire a management firm that likely would have charged us as much as 10 percent of the rent for services. That fee would have eaten into our cash flow and profit.

In fact, management costs can be sizeable for investors who own ten or fifteen homes spread out over a big city or county. TR is mindful of money, so he assumes management responsibilities for his single-family properties. If there is a problem with plumbing or a leaky roof, he must respond, no matter how early or late the hour. This saves money but eats up time.

What if my friend could own 100 homes in the same location though? Furthermore, what if all the problems encountered by renters could be easily and economically handled by trained management and tradespeople?

In this case, TR and other experienced investors like him would have only one job each month: to collect a nice check and deposit it in a bank account. *Sounds great, Thomas, but also complicated.*

If this is what you're thinking, you're probably not alone. Let me set your mind at ease on this point. Although many first-time investors are frightened by what they perceive as the complexity of real estate, in fact, the process can be grasped by understanding four basic principles:

1. Assets versus liabilities

2. Cash flow

3. Appreciation

4. Depreciation

Once you master these, you simply rinse and repeat. In doing so, you give yourself the opportunity to create a lucrative portfolio of hard assets, property, and a steady flow of passive income.

---

### *Passive Income Physician* takeaways!

- Find a mentor who can deepen your knowledge and confidence.

- Always have a plan, an end game that is easy to follow: Know your exit. Resist panic, even when markets rise and fall, which they inevitably will.

---

## SIX

# BUYING IN HOUSTON

Houston was not my place of residence when my family moved to east Texas, but it provided my next adventure in real estate. By 2009, the mortgage crisis had caused all kinds of harm in the general economy and torn asunder millions of families who lost their homes to foreclosure.

The damage was often the result of purchasing property at inflated prices, since everybody wanted a piece of the real estate boom, only for purchasers to soon discover that values had plummeted. Homeowners found themselves under water when a home

> in real estate you make your money on the buy, not the sell.

purchased for $395,000, for example, was suddenly worth only $259,000. It reminded me of yet another

43

adage: "In real estate, you make your money on the buy, not the sell." In other words, make sure you get a good price for the property.

Ironically, the financial wipeout created a buyer's market. No, the frenzy that preceded the downfall was *not* a buyer's market; even though everyone wanted in, it was truly a seller's market, and feverish bidding caused prices to soar. If you had a home to sell back then, you may have done very well.

Or, if you had access to financing, the aftermath likely provided you with an endless list of properties that sat empty in nice neighborhoods. Following our modest success in Indianapolis with the help of TR, Micaela and I were ready to take the next step, and it would be a somewhat aggressive move.

> For high-income professionals, net worth expands when we can take full advantage of the appreciation and depreciation of property that occurs over time.

For some investors, the concept of flipping homes had great allure, the ability to buy a bargain and quickly sell at a higher price. The novice imagines big, fast profits, pennies and dollars from Heaven, and I understand this impulse. Historically, the market provided a once-in-a-lifetime opportunity. The bubble had burst, and bargains were everywhere, yet there was not much competition because plenty of properties were available—a glut of them, in fact.

Regardless, flipping was not for me, nor should it be for any physician whose annual income puts him or her in the 40 percent tax bracket. Flipping homes for fast profit means the IRS will take a hefty piece of that pie. For high-income professionals, net worth expands when we can take full advantage of the appreciation and depreciation of property that occurs over time.

I fully embraced TR's wisdom: "You don't get rich selling real estate. You get rich *owning* real estate." Thus, Micaela and I began buying single-family homes that we could rent out. Guess who would want to move into our dwellings. Good people who, unfortunately, had lost their homes during the mortgage crisis. Remember this: When so-called bad things happen in the economy, it may create good opportunities for investors with available cash.

Since the drive to Houston was about ninety minutes from my home and I had a full-time job with a medical group, I often made deals sight unseen. The Internet allowed me to find beautiful homes that didn't need a lot of work, thus providing a big advantage over the properties featured on various reality TV shows, where the buyer dumps thousands of dollars into a renovation project to increase value and curb appeal.

With our income, we were eventually able to buy five homes in excellent neighborhoods. Since they were fairly new structures, maintenance was not a big deal. See how we built on our previous experience? That process went something like this:

- Initially, I was cautious about getting into real estate, and friends and family warned me against it. Finally, I overcame my doubts and bought a home just as the mortgage crisis was about to implode.

- We survived the crisis because we bought the home knowing we could afford our mortgage payments.

- We rented the home out to another family when my residency ended and we moved to Texas.

These simple steps involved risk and gave me confidence. If I had been a temporary owner of the Indianapolis home, a flipper, I would not have learned nor earned as much. When we sold the home, our profit was greater than it would've been, because for three years, someone else had paid the mortgage.

The process also allowed me to see how real estate could become a business, as long as I was willing to master basic concepts. What are these concepts?

Let's start with assets versus liabilities.

An asset is owned and expected to deliver economic benefits. Cash is an asset, as are inventory, equipment, land, and buildings, including multifamily apartment complexes. We need assets to build net worth, yet assets arrive with liabilities such as mortgage payments and services, which include all the responsibilities that come with providing shelter. Assets must exceed liabilities. Visualize your assets in one column and your liabilities in another. The difference between the two is your equity, the value you will receive after selling the asset (property) and paying all liabilities. There is another way to describe your equity: In truth, it is your net worth. Now let's create a real number for your eyes only. List your assets, jot down their value, and add that up. Do the same with your liabilities. Now you have two numbers, one larger than the other. Subtract liabilities, assuming that is the smaller figure, from assets, and you will arrive at a third number. This is the one you must grow to increase your net worth. Increased net worth is the key to retirement at any age. It will dictate a lifestyle of freedom and abundance or one of disappointment and meager living after retirement. How do you cultivate the net worth that will allow you to retire into a lifestyle you deserve and will be able to preserve with passive income? Consider this:

**Net Worth = Assets – Liabilities**

This simple formula is not something you do once, then stuff it into a digital file somewhere. Your net worth is a living organism. If you'll follow my *Passive Income Physician* takeaways, you'll see that the formula is an exercise you'll enjoy doing throughout the fiscal year. Seeing real growth that paper assets cannot possibly deliver is a stimulus to do more, to consider new opportunities and risks. A word of caution is in order here: Not everyone has a positive number in the beginning. If you recently finished your residency and you've borrowed six figures for your education, you already know you're under water, but it isn't because you've been a foolish spendthrift. Such a dire financial situation is common among doctors and other healthcare professionals.

As painful as it can be to contemplate and confront what feels like crippling debt, I'm offering you a way out. Merely working harder and longer to pay down loans can be draining. Considering multifamily and commercial property options, even in the beginning, with some help, can move you toward solvency, toward the place where you will have assets in excess of your liabilities.

I know, I know: The last thing you need after enduring a long training process is more training. So, look at it another way. Do the math and determine how long it will take to settle your debt. Then ask: *Is there a way I can get it done in half the time?*

New healthcare professionals just entering the field have an advantage over the doctors who have practiced for ten years and are still losing sleep over their negative net worth. By starting early and creating a plan for turning a bummer into a bonanza, the newbie can use time and planning to his or her advantage. There is one thing young and veteran physicians have in common: Both need to take dramatic steps to get out of debt. With that in mind, do the following:

- Work through the net worth formula, including every asset and liability.

- Create a budget that limits unnecessary outlay of cash.

- Dedicate larger and more frequent payments toward eliminating debt.

- Learn the lessons that can be used to transform bad debt into good debt.

Be careful. Debt consolidation may seem like a practical step. Having worked with one of America's largest banks during my student years, I can tell you that type of move may only increase the pain with higher interest payments, and that could add to the years you are in debt.

If you already have positive net worth but are

unhappy with the way your money is growing, you're in a great position: You have wealth that will allow you to consider a new class of assets, such as multifamily and commercial real estate. Making changes to your portfolio will certainly demand that you recalculate your net worth.

Embracing a broader economic perspective may also be useful. To some degree, we're all in this together. Where do you fit in? What is your age and income bracket? Economists measure the wealth of our nation by analyzing the net worth of the populace. By studying the average net worth of Americans, the U.S. Federal Reserve better understands the financial health of the nation. When markets such as housing and stocks hit a bump in the road, good people

**An asset puts money in your bank account. A liability pulls money out of your bank account**

like you, those who have holdings in those areas, also see a decline in value. Don't get down on yourself for things you cannot control. On the other hand, don't blindly follow the paper assets pack just because real estate seems like yet another educational mountain to climb.

By exploring the simple formula of assets versus liabilities, we begin to change our thinking, an essential part of expanding net worth. Believe me: My mind was awakened when I finally understood these simple principles:

a. An asset puts money in your bank account.

b. A liability pulls money out of your bank account.

Your relationship to assets and liabilities is changeable. When Micaela and I bought our home in Indianapolis, we may have thought we had an asset, but initially we had a liability. We had to make payments on a property that had lost value during the mortgage crisis.

Thanks to our mentor and friend TR, our home became an asset when we moved out and let another family move in, when their monthly rent became money in our bank account. We expanded on that strategy when we bought five homes in the Houston area and benefitted from tax laws that favor long-term holdings. So why did we decide to sell those properties five years later?

Bigger dreams began to bloom. The equity from the sale of our property provided the funding we needed to invest in new, larger projects. It was obvious by then that our net worth would expand exponentially if we upgraded our endeavor, but it wasn't merely a matter of a more favorable assets-versus-liabilities balance. Now, we were ready to master passive income concepts such as larger cash flow, appreciation, and depreciation. Although we took on more risk, we also put ourselves in the position of receiving greater gains that would brighten our future.

## Passive Income Physician takeaways!

- An asset must be owned and under your control before it creates economic benefits.

- Amounts of money that are owed to you may also be considered assets, such as monthly rent from each apartment dweller.

- In a sense, Airbnb has helped homeowners create a modest asset: They receive money for renting a room to visitors and vacationers.

- Acquiring multifamily properties creates a liability, the mortgage, while also providing an asset that creates income. When properly managed, it can be an asset that expands net worth.

## SEVEN

# FOLLOW YOUR HEART

If you don't do it right, being a doctor can be ruinous. The demands of the work can quickly deteriorate the body, mind, and soul. While in school, being smart was a huge asset, often all you needed to succeed; however, in real practice, possessing superior medical intelligence is not enough to ensure overall success as a physician. To be truly fulfilled, the healthcare professional must also be financially aware.

> To be truly fulfilled, the healthcare professional must also be financially aware

At the beginning of my story, I described two doctors: Dr. Desperate finds himself caught in a frightening but preventable predicament, and Dr. Bliss lives in abundance, but it took some discipline and desire to get there.

In reality, most of us fluctuate between the attitudes and experiences of both of these. We don't get it all right at the beginning of our careers; we make mistakes and fail to see the big picture. After climbing the mountain of a prolonged medical education, we would be wise to immediately give some consideration to our ultimate goals, but who has time for that?

Right out of residency, I was thrilled to join a busy medical group owned by physicians in east Texas. My hope was that I'd learn the ropes of operating a facility and one day grow my own business.

When I joined this democratically operated group, there were 18 doctors. They were well established and respected and had built a great practice together. For two years, I worked as an independent contractor. When I was finally offered partnership in the group, I was ecstatic and focused all my energy on making us better.

Meanwhile, I continued to pursue my real estate dreams, though my free time was minimal. As the years wore on, I learned a truth that we all have to live with: Health care is a dynamic industry, and the pressures of corporate politics and government regulations are physically and emotionally draining. As my enthusiasm waned, my views about my future—and my family's future, by then including Micaela and our four children—changed. In fact, the writing had been on the wall for quite some time, but I was too proud to admit it.

Basically, I had burned out from working too many hours, and I was missing my family. I was losing sight of why I joined the group in the first place.

Another issue began to cramp my style too. It is common among physicians, but in my opinion, it is also quite short-sighted. It is the demand that good doctors focus only on serving patients so they will never be distracted by outside interests, including my true passion: real estate. In Texas, free-standing emergency medicine facilities had begun to crop up like fast food franchises. Since they were not attached to hospitals, they did not have to play by the same rules. They were not required to accept healthcare insurance or Medicaid. They could turn away whomever they wished; in other words, people who could not pay cash received no care. The facilities were compact, about the size of an average hamburger outlet, and they were very profitable.

Could my team of skilled, dedicated physicians see ways to expand our business and income by owning such a business? Nope. This was entirely out of the question, because to do so would mean breaking away from our guiding principle: medicine only.

The day I decided to leave the group was one of the best and toughest days of my professional life. I had enormous respect for all my partners and had grown to love them like family. For that reason, the separation was agonizing in some ways, yet at the time, it was the correct decision for me, for Micaela, and for our children. Learn to follow your heart. It is a challenging but fulfilling life lesson.

But now what?

Most of my colleagues thought I was crazy when I solicited money to build an apartment community. As I mentioned earlier, I'd found a three-acre, correctly zoned lot in the middle of the city. The land, a foreclosure remnant, had been vacant for quite some time due to an oil pipeline that ran through the center of the property. By then, I'd decided to be bold and jump into the world of real estate, even if everyone thought I was nuts—everyone except my business partner. To buy the property, I needed my own investment capital. That was when Micaela and I decided to sell the five homes we were renting in Houston. It would be quite fair to ask, *"Why give up a good thing? If it was working for TR, why not you?"*

The answer is simple: Multifamily properties provide even bigger gains. If I own five houses and raise the rent by $100, I gain $500 per month. If I own a 50-unit property and raise the rent by $100, I gain $5,000 per month. I like that larger number but not for obvious reason. When we dig deeper and begin to grasp the glorious concept of appreciation versus depreciation, we realize there is far more than meets the eye in multifamily real estate.

First, keep in my mind that I'm not putting down ownership of single-family homes. The basic strategy of letting a renter pay your mortgage is powerful, but let's multiply that advantage.

Appreciation is almost self-explanatory. Over time, the property grows in value. Thus, the investor expands equity. Nice, right? Still, single-family homes and small multifamily homes—a duplex or four-unit property, for example—are appraised by comparing similar properties in the neighborhood.

Contrast that practice with appraisal of large multifamily properties, apartment complexes, which are considered commercial real estate. These valuations are determined by the money each property earns. The net operating income (NOI) is easy to figure: Just subtract all expenses from the property's gross income. When that number rises, which means your income is growing, the building appreciates, and that growth is not necessarily limited by other buildings in the neighborhood.

Improving the NOI of a multifamily property is not that difficult, but the outcome is profoundly better than fixing up a single-family dwelling. In the beginning, you can use these tried-and-true methods:

- Raise rent; this creates more income.

- Improve tenant retention so vacancies are rare. Create new services and amenities, such as covered parking.

- Decrease expenses by tracking every outgoing dollar.

A newly purchased multifamily property is not a static asset. You won't be stuck with the values. In fact, it is possible to *force* appreciation so the NOI grows automatically.

Again, by comparison, it is difficult to do the same with a single-family home. Sure, you can invest in a new kitchen, but how much must you raise the rent to pay for that improvement? Will the higher rate help or make it more difficult to rent the property?

To better understand why optimizing NOI improves the value of your multifamily property, look at the formula for calculating value of commercial real estate:

**Property Value = NOI / Capitalization Rate (Cap Rate)**

What does this mean? The equation tells us that the capitalization rate is the rate of return an investor can expect to receive if he or she paid all cash for a property. Cap rates are market specific; the cap rate depends on the various markets and submarkets around the country.

The examples below illustrate how commercial real estate is valued based on this income approach. Look at the example of a 10 percent cap rate market that increases the annual NOI of a 300-unit property from $1 million to $2.8 million. How's that for a leap in value?

Starting Value = $100,000 / 0.10% = $ 1,000,000

Improved Value = $280,000 / 0.10% = $ 2,800,000

That's a big increase, but how did we do it? We increased the rent by fifty dollars per unit. The math is simple: 300 units x $50 = $15,000 per month. Multiply $15,000 by 12 months, and you enjoy an added income of $180,000 annually, thereby increasing NOI by $180,000. This is how we can force appreciation and add $1.8 million in value.

Let's go further, all in pursuit of appreciation.

You can add more value by improving operations of a property or maxing them out. Again, the methods are standard. Conservation will reduce the water bill. Other cost-reduction steps include renegotiating all third-party contracts for utilities, trash pickup, and other services. Here's a creature comfort idea for adding revenue: Expand services for tenants. Human beings love helpful add-ons, such as the opportunity to pay a small monthly fee for covered parking, pet care, and other amenities. This, too, fits under the heading of forced appreciation, because it ultimately puts more money in your pocket.

Am I oversimplifying the concept of forced appreciation? Yes, to some degree. Various forces will determine property appreciation. Obviously, location of the property matters, as do wise management practices, but that does not mean you must only buy in the very best and most expensive neighborhoods. The goal is to improve properties so gross income can grow. Let's explore depreciation. To do so, we need to broaden this conversation to include multifamily tax benefits that help you retain hard-earned income, as this is an essential part of growing retirement accounts for highly taxed professionals.

When you own multifamily real estate, you receive preferential treatment. You read that correctly: Self-starters and highly taxed business owners get preferential tax advantages by owning multifamily and commercial real estate.

First, working people are taxed on their gross income, and taxes are taken out of paychecks automatically. This hurts, because it leaves those folks with less money to pay all their expenses.

That's not the case for real estate investors, even though we eventually build an incredible gross income that far exceeds the paychecks of most W-2 employees. We are entitled to deduct expenses, including mortgage interest, *before* paying taxes. The net result? Less money is taxed. Now, let's tackle depreciation, which can be a confusing concept. We naturally think in terms of growing things: business, family, and earning power. What's depreciation have to do with that, if anything?

In theory, everything we buy degrades or loses value as time goes on. A 1-year-old laptop is not worth what it cost when you bought it. The IRS recognizes this and, therefore, allows us to write off or depreciate assets over time. This is called a paper loss.

It is lawful to deduct this same loss in real estate. Investors subtract depreciation of property from the actual income of the multifamily property. In doing so, we decrease taxable income. Note that land does not depreciate; only the buildings on the property and all their components, such as windows, toilets, appliances, roofing, are subject to depreciation.

The significance of depreciation for investors can be seen when comparing a single-family home with a multifamily apartment building. Below, the first set of numbers is for a $100,000 single-family rental; the second refers to a $5 million apartment complex. For the purposes of this comparison, we will assume the value of the land to be worth 20 percent.

$$\text{Depreciation} = \$100,000 - (\$100,000 \times 0.20\%) =$$
$$\$80,000 \ / \ 27.5 \text{ years} = \$2,909$$

$$\text{Depreciation} = \$5,000,000 - (\$5,000,000 \times 0.20\%) =$$
$$\$4,000,000 \ / \ 27.5 \text{ years} = \$145,454$$

Allow me to boil this down: For each year of ownership, the real estate investor can deduct the above amounts (single family at $2,909 or multifamily at

$145,454) against respective property income, in addition to deducting the operating expenses. Obviously, there is a big difference between the two examples. For high-income professionals, the larger amount of depreciation is preferred. There is one more advantage though: Depreciation is described as a paper loss, as opposed to an actual loss of money, because investors are entitled to this tax break even when their multi-family properties are making money. Yes, that means they are *appreciating*.

I can assure you that this apparent paradox, this opportunity, is entirely legal and written into the tax code. The problem is that too many medical professionals are unaware that the laws of the land encourage us to build great wealth.

We're not done with this depreciation versus appreciation issue though. Once you subtract expenses and depreciation from gross receipts, you might still show a profit that the IRS will want to tax like ordinary income. Once again, believe it or not, tax laws come to our rescue, because they include a factor called *accelerated depreciation*. Here's how it works: Investors separate all non-structural elements of a property from the structure itself. Thus, first, the building gets depreciated at the rate I already defined. Then depreciation of its contents is accelerated, on a five-, seven-, or fifteen-year schedule. Obviously, this expands the investor's paper loss, so even less income is taxed.

An example of accelerated depreciation on personal taxes begins with the depreciation figure I shared above. Let's do the math on a seven-year schedule:

$$\text{Depreciation} = \$5,000,000 - (\$5,000,000 \times 0.20\%) =$$
$$\$4,000,000 / 27.5 \text{ years} = \$145,454$$

To accelerate, we must now divide the total depreciation amount of four million by seven years. That gives us $571,428, but what is the impact? The owner(s) of that property can write off another $571,428 of depreciation on tax returns for each of the 7 years. This significantly reduces the total income the IRS will tax.

These numbers impressed my friend and mentor, TR, yet he continues to make a compelling argument for starting in real estate that feels right and manageable for someone new to the industry.

On the flipside, experienced investors like TR might also consider expanding their portfolio by owning a 10 percent equity share in a property. Using the above example, the shareholder would decrease taxes by over $57,000 per year. If you are a physician or other professional who is in a 39 percent tax bracket, the accelerated 7-year depreciation schedule will put more than $22,000 back in your pocket! The benefit is yours, even if you are not the sole owner of this example of a multifamily property.

This is a lot of information to grasp, but my goal here is to provide you with an overview so you might better see the method to my madness. Yes, our single-family home investments were good to us. The learning process was significant, and it was my deepening involvement and love of real estate that made me realize I wanted to grow and expand net worth at a faster rate. In truth, I believed I had no choice but to go big and expand passive income, if my goal was to retire early from medicine or continue to practice on my own terms. I dreamt of making money work for me, not working to make money.

The only real difference between Dr. Desperate and Dr. Bliss is that one decided to take some financial risks in pursuit of ownership, while the other buried his head in the sand. Dr. Desperate was content being an employee and never owning anything that he would have the right to control and grow.

> **Making money work for me, not working to make money**

What about my esteemed colleagues, the naysayers who were confused by my decision to leave the medical group? Are they desperate or blissful?

A funny thing happened on my way to multifamily wealth: My former teammates began to see the light. Eventually, as a group, they changed their policies and invested in real estate, including establishing a few of those free-standing emergency medicine operations I described.

Hey, no hard feelings here; only hard assets. That's the path to true wealth.

## Passive Income Physician takeaways!

- Learn to follow your heart. No guts, no glory.

- Examine your current investment strategy. I moved beyond single-family after crunching the numbers. Always crunch the numbers.

- Consider investments that don't demand that you shoulder the full burden of ownership. Buying a share of multifamily with the right firm can be a profitable and educational endeavor.

# EIGHT

# WHAT'S THE CATCH?

By now, it should be apparent that passive income wealth is not derived merely by buying and selling property and making a huge profit. No, it's about the lucrative tax advantages available to multifamily investors that compound the gains. These lawful write-offs all but demand that high-income professionals get involved, especially when considering the alternative: Low-yield investments offer no tax advantage, as there is no overhead involved. Unless the physician owns the building that houses his or her private practice, what can he or she deduct from income beyond those lab coats and stethoscopes? The truth is that most self-employed people without ten years of education have more tax breaks than doctors.

Most of my colleagues in the medical group were in that same boat, in that they had no overhead because we were all third-party contractors with local hospitals. As you now know, the group did not wish to invest, so they did not own tangibles that could depreciate. Instead, all the income derived from billing hospitals for services was passed on to the doctors, some of whom may have earned over $600,000 per year. That sounds good, right? That's a lot of money, but what did they do with it? Millennial high-income earners in the medical profession typically max out their retirement accounts, even though those benefits cannot compare to the net worth expansion that comes with real estate. To repeat a previous equation, setting aside $50,000 per year, multiplied by 20 years equals $1 million. That's not enough for a long and happy retirement though. Some very rich doctors go to extremes and buy overpriced homes with no cash flow, in a misguided effort to harvest tax write-offs on a losing proposition. Does that make sense? Absolutely not. The cardinal rule for passive income physicians is this: Only buy properties with guaranteed positive yields.

But there is a catch. Fortunately, there is also an easy way to resolve it.

To be considered a professional who is eligible for all these benefits, the IRS rules state that you must be active in the operation of your property. Only people who can claim a minimum of 750 hours per year in hands-on involvement get 100 percent of the tax breaks, while everyone else is limited to deducting interest, etc., from property income.

This requirement understandably makes most physicians groan. They are too busy, and possibly fed-up with all the regulatory demands that come with joining the medical profession. They will complain louder when I say, "Hey, all you have to do is become a licensed mortgage broker or realtor."

But what if your spouse had time to earn the credential? That is how Micaela and I earned our tax breaks. My lovely wife and mother of our four children went through the licensing process so we could make the best of our real estate investments when we began buying homes in Houston in 2010. It was part of the plan when we moved to east Texas. I certainly didn't have spare hours after hiring on with the medical group, then becoming a partner. At first, I was concerned that it might be too demanding for her while our children were young.

"Would you mind doing all that studying?" I asked, well aware that she had been a diligent and successful student at the University of North Texas.

"Why would I mind? With all the work you do for our family, how could I not want to help you? I want to contribute."

That was a sweet moment. It reinforced that we were on the same page and shared a passion for growth. It proved to me that expanding our net worth to create financial stability was not a wild, extravagant plan embraced only by the mad doctor in the family.

Micaela's eagerness to be involved also meant we could spend more time together, visiting properties and meeting with the managers we'd hired to maintain those complexes. This allowed us to remain close, while also contributing to the annual hours the license required. It certainly wasn't all fun and games. To this day, my industrious wife continues to study to improve her knowledge of real estate and will eventually add other licenses to her credential.

> **The engaged professional who asks for assistance is more likely to get on the path to incredible wealth because shared burdens and ownership are the norm, a means to an end.**

The passive income physician is not an island or unwilling to delegate tasks. The engaged professional who asks for assistance is more likely to get on the path to incredible wealth because shared burdens and ownership are the norm, a means to an end. If you don't have a significant other to help you expand your financial playing field, I stress that there are various methods for creating streams of passive revenue. My choice is multifamily and commercial real estate because each property Micaela and I buy is a business, yet these businesses do not require that I run them alone.

Where else does this opportunity exist? Could

you consider purchasing a fast-food or oil lube franchise? Sure, and some business people have done very well acquiring those types of assets, but I know nothing about those sectors and the shops cannot operate on autopilot. I'd lose my shirt for sure!

Acquiring multifamily and commercial real estate properties, on the other hand, is a business model that can be repeated endlessly. Learn from the purchase of one property, then purchase the next with the pretax money you retained, thanks to IRS rules that benefit multifamily investors.

To repeat: One key to success is being willing to rely on the talent and time of others. Micaela has played a pivotal role in our ability to confidently travel down the ever-widening road to passive income wealth, and more teachers and creative go-getters would soon contribute to our expansion.

## Passive Income Physician takeaways!

- Physicians must invest so annual deductions allow them to keep more of the money they earn.

- Your most important business partner may be your spouse. Plan together.

- Passive income wealth can be created by buying businesses you will own but won't have to operate yourself.

NINE

# FAMILY OWNED

Before I made the leap from single-family to multifamily and commercial real estate, I experienced a revelation that made my head spin. It all seemed to be inspired by the geographic change my family and I made when we left Indiana.

My wife has family in Texas, so that was a factor in accepting a position with the medical group I eventually left, after toiling for more than half a decade. Being close to our roots, our family, is a good thing.

But it was not familiarity that transformed my thinking. Moving to the easterly section of the Lone Star State was like stepping back in time. The business lifestyle was from another era. Many establishments were family owned; chain restaurants and Big Box corporate entities were at a minimum as compared to other parts of the country. What stunned me the most was that many people who were born in the area returned after college to raise their families and make their mark in the communities where they grew up. In fact, many never went to college at all.

After notching a subpar high school academic track record, I'd spent more than two decades in the Navy and medical school in pursuit of a highly skilled position that I hoped would help me fulfill my purpose in life and support my family. These were all good motives, admirable goals, and I would not trade my trajectory for anything.

Yet I had to wonder. My so-called high-bracket income as a physician was dwarfed by the money earned by the east Texans who had only a basic education. Electricians, plumbers, and gas station owners all made millions. And the lucrative income they received was the result of owning a business rather than labor at a job for someone else. While I was sailing the high seas, they had figured out that there is a better way to create wealth. In my opinion, that made my neighbors exceptionally smart. Street smart? Sure, that could describe their intelligence. Or salt-of-the-earth smart. Call it what you will, but after a long journey through the Seven Seas and the odyssey of medical school, I felt like an idiot. *Why had I decided to become a doctor? To impress somebody? To right the listing ship of my unexceptional performance in early life?*

Take note, my much-admired medical colleagues:

Education takes many forms. Yes, I know my east Texas mentors could not successfully or safely perform surgery, prescribe drugs, or endure a twenty-four-hour shift in an emergency medical facility.

But they were wealthy in a way that made me reconsider my future. They owned each day of their lives because they owned businesses. Essentially, they were already financially free.

> **Take note, my much-admired medical colleagues: education takes many forms.**

I met Pike Blakely when Micaela and I were looking to build our first home. He was an experienced custom builder, but after many conversations, I learned that his first love was owning and operating real estate. Only a few years earlier, Pike had earned his living as an electrician wiring homes. He had also managed to build several duplexes and found an opportunity to purchase and develop a large lot of 120 units in Marshall, Texas. He believed the property, if successful, might finally allow him to break free from his day job. There was only one problem: Pike didn't have the money.

Fortunately, he was creative. Since that was before the mortgage crisis, when institutions were more lenient with their money, Pike eventually found a real estate investment trust (REIT) that would loan him more than half a million dollars, about 60 percent of the financing he needed. Typically, a REIT is a firm that owns and operates commercial properties that generate income, including multifamily. Some also provide financing for real estate.

The loan was a major building block but did not seal the deal, so Pike went to the owner of the property and negotiated seller financing. This allowed him to bypass another lending institution. The seller took out a second mortgage, about 20 percent of the total value, to help the transaction happen.

Why would a seller do such a thing? He would land the sale he wanted and make more money. By holding the mortgage for a defined period, perhaps a couple years, he would receive interest on the money he had loaned to Pike and the payback was guaranteed.

Pike's ingenuity launched him to success, and his hard-headed goal to live on passive income inspired me to think bigger. Suddenly, those five homes Micaela and I owned and rented seemed like stepping stones to larger possibilities.

Yet it took another east Texas native, though, to provide the vision necessary to buy the downtown property called Longview, the one that would be my first multifamily deal.

Steve Oram was a firefighter who also had been building custom homes for over twenty-five years. He knew that the property we wished to buy and develop had been ignored by other real estate investors because the oil pipeline that ran through the property created some zoning restrictions, the R-word that scared most people away. To make the land viable, we had to design buildings that conformed to the land, thereby satisfying the city's environmental concerns.

Not every project will come to you in perfect condition. The key to success is often in the creativity that enables you to see beyond roadblocks. We accepted the obvious challenges because we had a strategy. Unfortunately, even with all the careful planning we did for Longview, we could not anticipate every obstacle. Once construction began, we encountered setbacks. Yet each time one came along, we put our minds together with our architects, engineered a solution, and soldiered on. Quitting was not an option. After all, I'd nervously signed my name on the loan contract with the banker, after he noticed my hesitation and assured me, "You'll make money, son." What he might have added was, *"But it won't be easy."*

Although Longview, a small, sixteen-unit complex, took us nearly a year to finish and may have taken ten years off my life, I consider it to be one of my greatest achievements. Although I shared ownership with Steve, I tripled the number of units in my real estate portfolio, and I was now eligible for the substantial tax benefits I mentioned in the previous chapter. Graduating from medical school and becoming a board-certified emergency medicine physician was, of course, a great accomplishment too. But I'd already begun to see that being a doctor can be ruinous to body and soul. And, sad to say, it's not enough to be smart, even *really* smart. To survive, healthcare professionals must learn to take good care of themselves, all while fulfilling the Hippocratic Oath. Perhaps that is why developing real estate was gratifying in ways that I hadn't expected. It was the kind of self-care that moved me away from the fate of Dr. Desperate and toward the abundance of Dr. Bliss.

There was more though. In one fell swoop, I helped to create a place where people could live, work, and thrive. Knowing that put frosting on the cake, and it was a sweet sensation.

### Passive Income Physician takeaways!

- Partner with experienced people who share your ambition to live in abundance.

- Creativity is as important as crunching numbers. Learn to see through the obvious limitations of a property.

- Explore financing by talking with professionals who have experience with all the variables. Perhaps there are paths to success that you have not even considered or have yet to learn.

- The range between Dr. Desperate and Dr. Bliss is a spectrum. Imagine your life moving toward a more pleasing, abundant reality.

# TEN

# To Manage or *Not* To Manage

If you build it, will tenants come and want to live in your property? Maybe. The challenges were enormous when designing and constructing that first property, yet the gratification of making something far outweighed the grievances. When that new building is standing, it will be cause for celebration. Then you realize you have only crossed the desert. Now, you must climb the mountain.

When a new structure rises, people take notice. They drive or walk by, inquire about it, Google it, or mention it to friends. Businesses in the neighborhood will also be curious. This type of word-of-mouth is useful. Take every bit of "heard it through the grape-vine" attention you can get. There's no such thing as bad publicity, or so they say. Then get to work on your advertising plan.

Once tenants begin applying for the units you have created, they must be interviewed, background and credit checks must be processed, and rental agreements must be signed. What's that sound like to you?

To me, it seemed like a lot of work, piled on top of all the work we had already done to make the property available, not to mention the financial outlay and oversite.

To manage your own properties or not to manage your own properties? That is the question. It comes with a lot of responsibilities and tasks, all of them time consuming. Micaela and I had managed five single-family homes and done a good job of it, but did I find myself serving as Mr. Fix-it, strapping on my tool belt and always running out to repair leaky faucets or other assorted malfunctions? Of course not. I was a full-time doctor.

We delegated those needs to capable contractors, plumbers, electricians, and landscapers. We needed a crew to keep us in business, in the same way families might hire someone to mow the lawn or babysit the kids.

Not that you can't or shouldn't consider managing your own property. TR, my mentor and friend in Indianapolis, performed many of the management chores associated with his real estate because his schedule was more flexible than that of most nine-to-fivers. So, he could handle the workload.

Managing a multifamily housing complex was another matter. Consider the basic tasks:

- Define policies for rentals. What types of restrictions do you favor? No smoking or no pets are common. If you allow pets, how many and what kind?

- The types of tenant-screening you use and the vetting procedures you employ must be fair, consistent, and legal.

- Maintenance responsibilities may seem obvious but will require a plan, a routine that keeps every inch of the property clean. A walkthrough schedule is important and often allows you to make repairs before tenants complain.

- Response to tenant concerns and complaints must be timely. Returning phone calls or responding to tenants' letters is time consuming but essential. At times, it is necessary to send written response to clarify rental terms. Some delays may render you vulnerable to legal problems.

- A plan for managing emergency repairs must be established, because these will happen, even in new properties.

- Disaster protection must be considered, in the event of fire, flooding, and threatening weather. Create evacuation procedures that can be shared with tenants in writing.

- Safety equipment such as smoke alarms must be checked on a regular basis to be sure it will function when needed.

- Be proactive when it comes to pest infestations. In a new property, this will not likely be an immediate problem. Don't let it become a grievance.

- Educate tenants about all of the above, and make sure to put it all in writing and gather signatures to acknowledge understanding.

Clearly, the size of the property and the number of units may up the game. My first property only consisted of sixteen units, but each of our tenants had expectations. We had to communicate with them and deliver services.

Are you now ready to abandon this, to reject this method of expanding your net worth? Don't, and here is why.

Physicians have ample experience when it comes to marshaling resources and delegating responsibilities. As a manager of emergency medical facilities, I know I cannot do everything. I need nurses, other doctors, administrators, and managers. The team collaborates to make services available in critical situations and to keep the department functioning properly. Since we have those skills in our toolboxes, let's put them to good use in our new vocation as real estate investors.

Ideally, a multifamily community will have an onsite manager to handle day-to-day repairs and maintenance. Multifamily dwellings are really a social science experiment that demands a keen eye for detail and a willingness to act when problems threaten quality-of-life standards. The bottom line is apparent: Poor management can harm your rental income and may lead to lawsuits from tenants, all of which could reduce the market value of your real estate.

**Physicians have ample experience marshalling resources and delegating responsibility.**

We hire property managers because we cannot effectively run our growing real estate investments without help. But we must be diligent for all the reasons listed above; much is at stake. That said, we do not hire individuals but depend instead on firms that specialize in this type of management.

Saving time is one of the most attractive benefits

of hiring a management firm. The long but incomplete list above is proof that there are many demands associated with multifamily ownership.

Responding to tenants is the next best aspect of this hire. It's a tough job to answer every call concerning repairs, noise complaints, and so forth. Good management firms are experienced in objectively handling disputes. They remain fair but detached, unlike owners, who may take criticisms personally. Good management will also have a grasp of tenant-landlord legal issues and understand relations with the broader residential and business community.

Other beneficial skills may include accounting, leasing, and marketing savviness. A low vacancy rate is ideal, yet turnover is a fact of life. Skill at increasing income while lowering operating expenses is also a boon. Remember that any insightful suggestion may save you big bucks. In general, fees for property management companies range from 5 percent to 10 percent of the rent for each unit in your building or complex. This is an important addition to your assets versus liabilities chart. You must spend on services, yet you shouldn't do so at just any price. The management fee decreases when you buy property with at least fifty units. Larger properties make it practical for management firms to create an onsite office, which saves time and money. Under these circumstances, expect fees to be in the realm of 2.5 to 3.0 percent. Autopilot is not quite what you should expect from your relationship with the management firm. As a physician, you are used to having some say in the formulation of protocols and procedures, and the same is true in the real estate environment. It is perfectly acceptable for you to determine, for example, how often the manager firm reports to you. Set these expectations early in the relationship by including them in the contractual agreement.

Medical practices are more prone to succeed when solid systems are established, and the same holds true in your real estate ventures. As I've already made clear, many healthcare professionals are not necessarily good money managers, but that does not mean we cannot bring our skills from that profession into our growing empire of multifamily assets. Lean on your strengths but do not believe your so-called weaknesses demand that you have no say in how things are done.

A good example is leasing and marketing reports. Weekly updates will keep you abreast of leasing activities and rent collection. Details about new tenants can be useful as well; this may include the type of unit, such as one or two bedrooms; move-in date; length of lease and expiration date; amount of rent; and added fees tacked on for those extras we mentioned before, such as covered parking, storage, or pet services. Is this too much information? That is for you to decide.

Helpful reports will also enlighten you about marketing activities. What media was used to market the property? What were the results? Staying current on the competitive rental market is important too. If comparable properties are increasing rent and utility fees, maybe you should too.

Problems with rent collection is another important detail. The monthly checks from tenants is your cash flow. If your income stream is blocked due to late payments, you need to correct the problem before it does serious harm to your ability to pay monthly liabilities.

An annual budget forecast keeps everyone on track, as it projects income and expenses for the upcoming twelve months. Think of this as monitoring the wellbeing of a patient. After performing surgery or prescribing medication, doctors project a timeframe and quality of recovery. It is important to know if things are proceeding as expected or if there are setbacks. Real estate is also a living organism, and you should keep an eye on its progress.

Needless to say, there are warning signs if your management firm is not performing up to the standards set forth in your contract. Poor rent collection or high rates of delinquency should not be tolerated. No doubt, you will not be happy to receive a cash call requesting extra funds to cover operating expenses, because that is what the rent is for.

Bear in mind that online access to your property reports can save time and paper. Digital editions allow you to use whatever free minutes you have at the office to check in and remain a conscious participant in your goal to expand net worth.

You are the boss. You set the tempo of acquisition, the culture of your business enterprise, and the efficiency that suits your needs. It is likely that you've already honed most of these qualities, but by applying them to a new endcavor, you blend the confidence of a seasoned professional with the enthusiasm and curiosity of a student.

## *Passive Income Physician* takeaways!

- Delegate authority without losing command of your empire.

- Define a new contractual relationship early so it does not require serious revisions later.

- Exploit skills you have already developed, regardless of the weaknesses you think you have.

- Although your time may be limited, your authority is not. You are the boss. Your new business is your risk, responsibility, and reward.

# ELEVEN

# No Turning Back

When I made the decision to leave my partnership with the medical group and venture into multifamily real estate, I faced the proverbial question: *What's next?* Taking massive action had helped me through my time in the Navy and medical school. Now, I was ready to apply the same methods to the ultimate freedom of passive income, but it didn't play out as I expected.

During my time with the medical group, I did a good job of recruiting new physicians, which helped maintain high standards and keep the business stable. Also, my colleagues understood that I had a strong grasp of finance and the management of assets.

Prior to leaving the group, I was introduced to a physician who truly embodied Dr. Bliss. Unlike the other doctors I knew, he was an investor and medical director of a regional system and managed several hospitals. The firm had recapitalized, which created a lot of cash for investors. With so much money on hand, this Dr. Bliss saw no reason to continue working clinically every day. In short, I was offered the opportunity to replace him, albeit gradually, so he could spend more time where he really wanted to be, out on his sailboat.

Does this sound like a contradiction, replacing one employment position with another, while professing the goal of owning my own time? In a way, it is, but that offer provided a unique opportunity to add income that could be earmarked for more real estate. Also, when I accepted the offer in late summer, I managed only one facility, not a full workload. It did, however, demand my attention because I could see immediately that standards had to be upgraded. I commenced with weeding out poor-performing doctors and replacing them with top-quality professionals. By the following spring, I was managing all eight hospitals. Here again, this may seem like a compromise. Why would I take on even more responsibility?

In truth, it was difficult to turn away the income, especially since my real estate venture was a fairly new passion. I had concerns, and the Longview project was not exactly a walk in the park.

For starters, accepting the new position meant moving to the Dallas-Fort Worth area. That was fine with us, because the larger city meant new and bigger real estate opportunities. Although we'd increased our net worth by several million dollars, there were still gaps in my knowledge. To enhance and speed up the learning cycle, I joined a real estate group and attended as many seminars as I could; if doctoral degrees were awarded merely for the willingness to absorb more information, I would have been a prime candidate. I attended events, shook a lot of hands, and sought new relationships.

Throughout my introduction to Dallas, I no longer had to listen to physicians and other colleagues question the sanity of my real estate ambition. Instead, Micaela assumed that role. "You're crazy," she said often, and I can't blame her.

I lived, breathed, and bled real estate. If we were on the beach or enjoying some other vacation destination with the kids, all the while, I'd assess the local real estate, make phone calls, or dream up new plans for expanding our net worth. Yes, I sacrificed some quality time with family—not to mention the pleasure of a beautiful shoreline—but I was doing my best to take control of my destiny, using my free time as I pleased, and it never felt like work.

Contrast that with the vacations I pined for and desperately needed for recovery while working all those nights amidst the emergency room chaos, in the wee hours, dealing with coughs, sore throats, fevers, and gunshot wounds. Honestly, I remain eternally grateful that I earned a credential that allowed me to serve my community, and I cherish the many meaningful experiences I had throughout my tenure. The problem was the deep fatigue, the physical and soulful deterioration induced by the work.

Physicians often don't want to think about retirement because they love ministering to people in need and don't really have a plan for the day when they don't have doctors anymore. Sometimes, though, I wonder if the term limits some politicians face shouldn't be applied to healthcare professionals. Put in your time, do good work, and be proud. Then, let the next wave of idealists carry the torch so you don't have to limp to the finish line of life.

As for Dallas, my determination to create new relationships paid off when I finally connected with a couple businessmen who not only shared my enthusiasm but had already accomplished much of what I was trying to do. All I had learned while developing the Longview property— zoning, utilities placement, engineering, environmental protection, etc.— was now necessary in my pursuit to acquire funding for my most ambitious financial deals to date.

My new colleagues enlightened me about syndicators and private placement memorandums.

A real estate syndicator, or syndication, is a promoter of real estate deals. It may be a corporation, a limited liability company (LLC), or a firm with full or limited partnerships. Essentially, they crowdfund to raise about 25 percent of the value of the property they wish to buy. Many passive income physicians may not have time to search for diamonds in the rough, so the syndicate provides deals to consider.

If you choose to use a syndicator, be careful in choosing. Study the track record of the group. You must feel comfortable with the business practices and integrity of whomever you work with. Ideally, you know someone who is personally involved or can recommend the firm.

I learned a great deal by working with a regionally known multifamily syndicator, and the big picture quickly came into full view. The final piece to the puzzle was my introduction to the private placement memorandum (PPM). It sounds fancy, but it's really little more than a securities offering, a legal document that sets forth the terms of a deal offered to potential private investors. Like a stock offering that seeks to raise private equity from accredited investors, the PPM must be filed with the Securities Exchange Commission (SEC).

A PPM is a simple document to create, but there are strict guidelines. Defining risk comprises a large portion of it. It also describes the multifamily property to be bought, outlines the business plan, and includes the biographies of those people who are making the offer. The document also requires investors to answer questions to define the breadth of their wealth. The onus for reviewing credentials falls to the syndicators.

An example of a PPM would be the opportunity to buy shares in a real estate deal at $1,000 per share with a minimum investment of 50 shares. Where do the investors get the $50,000? Self-directed IRAs and 401(k) s, retirement vehicles, are often used for this purpose.

I'd come a long way from wanting to buy my own home while still a medical student, but here's some good news for you: The path I took *is* possible for many physicians with a yearning for passive income.

That is why I cannot stress enough the value of believing in yourself. All it takes is choosing a direction and beginning. You will make mistakes, just as I have and still will, but these errors will be the best learning experiences of your life.

### *Passive Income Physician* takeaways!

- My path to passive income was not a straight line. Be flexible. Consider all opportunities that come your way.

- Whenever you see a gap in your knowledge, be confident that someone in the profession can help, if you'll only reach out and network.

- Define what wealth means to you. Then, search for a Dr. Bliss among your circle of colleagues and model yourself after him or her.

- Consider using 401(k) or self-directed IRA funds to invest in real estate ventures via private placement memorandums (PPMs).

TWELVE

# Rolling It Over

The Longview project took one year to complete. Despite the challenges, I was proud of the accomplishment, but it was no time to get sentimental. Within eighteen months, my partners and I decided to sell the complex.

This may seem like yet another contradiction, one that went against the sage advice of my brilliant friend TR who declared so often that you make money in real estate through ownership. Holding on to property that creates generous passive income will always be a wise choice, but we had our reasons for offering the property when we did.

A lot of multifamily units had been constructed to satisfy the need for housing during an oil boom. That's Texas for you. As the excitement tapered off, we feared that a glut of apartments in a small town would harm our ability to maintain or expand revenue from rent.

Fortunately, we had some equity in the property and sold at a profit. In hindsight, it was a good move, because over the next several years, the property sold three more times and with each transaction the valuation decreased. We took a gamble and won.

The Longview project is a good example of looking beyond your pride and joy, that beautiful property you developed, and recognizing larger economic and social trends. You won't always get it right. How many investors have liquidated an asset, only to see prices fly? They probably regret missing out on more profit. Still, you don't want to be on the losing end of predicting value shifts.

Moreover, we didn't take the sales profit and sit back and gloat. Our strategy was to use that money to invest in other properties that would help expand net worth. We put the funds to work by purchasing several commercial properties in Kilgore, Texas, light industrial warehouses that were not such a far cry from multifamily. We still receive rent from tenants, and the cash flow has been quite good.

There is, however, an important issue embedded in the sale of one property and the purchase of others: taxation. After a sale, the law says we must account for all the depreciation and accelerated depreciation we took advantage of through the years, then pay capital gains taxes.

Paying the piper hurts profit, doesn't it?

Subtract Uncle Sam's piece of the action, and we have less to work with, right?

Yes, but we can defer taxes and keep that money on the sale of multifamily properties. Eventually, when all is said and done, somewhere down the road, we'll pay taxes; they don't just disappear. Wouldn't it be so much better, though, if we could withhold those pay-outs to our government, buy more property, earn more revenue, make more profit, then pay up? The Internal Revenue Code Section 1031, also known as like-kind exchanges, gives us that option, allowing us to hold on to our money when we exchange one property for another. That was precisely what we did with our Longview property: we used that money to buy other properties.

There are some rules, of course. Exchanged property must be "similar in character, nature or class to qualify," according to the IRS. But those distinctions are flexible. The laws allowed us to exchange Longview for commercial property, or we could have purchased a vacant lot if we preferred. We were not allowed to exchange for ineligible assets such as inventory, stocks and bonds, securities and debt, and certificates of trust.

Some experienced real estate investors go even further and legally exploit the 1031 exchange code. For example, they may refinance a commercial building, then use the equity to buy even more property. Time restrictions apply, and the 1031 tax exchange is available only for business and investment properties, not your primary residence or vacation home, but eligibility includes individuals, corporations, partnerships, trusts, and LLCs. Keeping the money so it can do more good work for you is the essence of the passive income physician. By using pretax dollars, we buy more assets, thus expanding net worth. The 1031 exchange advantages encourage us to always be looking for opportunities. You never know when you might find real estate that can be added to or exchanged for property in your portfolio. Think of it as a sports team that is seeking ways to improve performance. Through the years, some fans are shocked when popular and gifted athletes suddenly are sent to another team in exchange for other talent. Not every trade works, but the goal is always the same: to add value.

The dynamics of trade, of exchanges, continue to intrigue me. On one hand, we were fortunate to sell the Longview complex at the top of the market. We know that to be true because the value has since dropped significantly. On the other hand, we must also look for multifamily or commercial properties that have been neglected and present a buy-low scenario.

In downtown Fort Worth, there is a thriving arts district near Texas Christian University. Buying property in the epicenter of that activity might not make sense because inflated prices could make it difficult to turn a profit. Thus, we widened our search to the outskirts of the area and found a twenty-one-unit multifamily building. It was built in the 1970s and had fallen into disrepair, despite its close proximity to an attractive community and residential neighborhoods where single-family homes routinely sell for $700,000 or more.

Although it was small, by completely renovating the building for young professionals, we put ourselves in the position of benefitting from the sprawl of the economically robust arts district. Is this building a long-term keeper? I can only say that we'll remain alert for whatever is best for improving passive income and net worth.

This venture does have some similarity to the Longview project. At the time, nobody wanted to buy that piece of land because of the environmental complications. Perhaps the sweet Fort Worth building was passed over because it obviously needed some work.

Your interests or insights may differ from mine, and that's fine. The beauty of real estate is that there is something for everyone.

Even so, we can agree that by looking for bargains and understanding the tax implications of real estate transactions, every medical professional has a shot at creating an abundant retirement portfolio.

## *Passive Income Physician* takeaways!

- Love the concept of passive income accumulation more than you love any one multifamily or commercial property.

- Pretax dollars are a welcome and necessary element of building massive wealth.

- The least attractive properties only make sense if analysis proves that they can provide positive revenue, month after month.

# THIRTEEN

# MANAGING ASSETS

You might be wondering how I got my hands on that Fort Worth property. I know what you're thinking: *Does this guy really have that kind of money lying around after so few years investing in real estate?* No, but it wasn't *my* money. It was the money of investors who understood the essential need for passive income.

Despite the success Micaela and I enjoyed in our initial single-family and multifamily investments, I knew we could do more if we reached beyond our own resources, if we used a combination of income, investments, and bank loans to engage a larger circle of like-minded investors.

Dallas was an awakening, because the relationships I was fortunate to cultivate showed me a bigger world. Once that happened, I pushed through doors that previously seemed like walls. Yes, some of the self-doubt

I learned as an under-performing high school student continued to linger.

Suddenly, I stepped into a whole new arena, a place where money was no problem. Believe me when I tell you that there really is a lot of money out there looking for a home.

After learning about syndicates and PPMs, the next step was obvious. I knew I had the ambition, drive, and contacts to create my own asset management firm. This meant I could create a team of professionals whose specialties gave us keen advantages in the marketplace. We could raise money, much more than Micaela and I had, and with it provide an investment opportunity to my tribe: physicians and other professionals who earned a high income but needed their money to grow significantly from year to year.

> **Investing is not only about having a lot of money.**

That Fort Worth property was within reach, and it was fairly easy to convince investors that that relatively small property was a solid investment. Why? Because I leveraged much more than money. I expanded on my own knowledge by attracting other talented, experienced people. We gained strength by teaming up. Together, we had a lot to offer novice and veteran real estate investors alike. Through effective networking, we had education, encouragement, analysis, and a sound financial plan. The success of an asset management firm is in its ability to leverage everyone's skill set.

Might you eventually create your own firm? Absolutely. If that is your goal, I'll be the first to cheer and congratulate you, but do you have the resources to go it alone?

I've already mentioned that by starting my own company, I no longer leveraged money only. I also took full advantage of the collective skills and intelligence of our group, but there is one more area we must all expand if we intend to prosper: time.

Do you have enough hours in your day to do it all? This is not a question of intelligence or street smarts; rather, it is a practical matter of physical and mental endurance. If I can call on a colleague to track down and analyze properties that will turn a profit, I have gained a lot, even though I may not own 100 percent of that asset.

It's not that different from a hospital. The institution hires gifted people who share the wealth of their skills and medical creativity so everyone who walks in the door benefits. A synergy develops, so much so that the whole is greater than the sum of its partners.

Investing is not just about having a lot of money, nor is it only about your connections. Rather, it is the ability to harness and then multiply the power your community brings to the game.

Who should you include on your team? Let me provide a short list:

- Contract attorney

- Securities Exchange Commission (SEC) attorney

- A management company to analyze and underwrite investments

- Insurance expert

- A CPA familiar with depreciation as it pertains to taxation

How do you assemble your team? Choose wisely. Personal and professional integrity is key. Résumés will tell you about the past, but where do your team members want to go? What are their goals and ambitions? Building passive income to expand net worth through multifamily and commercial real estate is my mission, so I seek like-minded people, and so should you.

There is another group of players that might not formally be considered teammates but are still helpful. When analyzing potential markets, for example, it is important to know if rent is increasing, stable, or declining. What is the history of the neighborhood you are considering? Has it been gentrified, or is it on the verge of that kind of change? With so much information to gather, you'd be wise to have people on the ground who understand the areas of a city or town that you find interesting.

That same need expands when your team begins exploring presumably hot real estate communities, such as Atlanta, Phoenix, and various cities in the Midwest. Can you or your team members keep a close watch on all those places? You need to stay on top of developing trends, and the more eyes you can engage, the better. These may only be acquaintances. Even a cold call to a dweller in the area could offer insight that will shape your informed decision.

One sign your team should look for is relocation or expansion of large businesses in the area. General Motors recently added thousands of jobs in Arlington, Texas, near a 300-unit community we own. Those employees will need housing. The construction or reopening of a plant is a tip that something significant may be happening. Often, this is how it goes: new infra-structure, more jobs, and a necessity for housing. Also, operating in a state that is friendly to landlords should go without saying, but I'm saying it anyway.

Do not make the mistake of thinking building a team is only for companies that intend to build portfo-lios full of large properties. All of the above also per-tains to real estate investors who only wish to concen-trate on four- and eightplexes. As I mentioned, in the beginning, Micaela and TR in Indianapolis were my very important teammates.

Even after organizing your team and doing all I've suggested, don't think you'll always win. There is a lot of money out there, but the good deals can be competitive. In a sense, the asset firm must audition for the seller. We put hours of planning into an offer that begins with submitting a letter of intent (LOI), wherein we outline the terms for purchase. This is not a binding contract, as the nitty-gritty details will be worked out when negotiating a purchase and sale agreement (PSA).

Just because I'm passionate about multifamily and commercial real estate, that does not mean I am unique, particularly now. We have reached a point where rent is soaring in some cities, which means the best buildings are showing nice profits. This makes owners wonder if now is a good time to sell, just as I sold my Longview complex at the top of the market. Not only that, but there are numerous buyers out there. Therefore, we're in an unusual situation where the market is advantageous for both sellers and buyers. A lot of smart money is changing hands in the zeal for hard assets.

> A lot of smart money is changing hands in the zeal for hard assets.

The rush to acquire real estate puts pressure on my team. Choosing the right properties and making attractive offers are crucial. When things don't go our way, such as when we lose out on a fifteen million-dollar property, it can be frustrating.

This is why mindset continues to be so important. In the beginning, you must clear your head of negative thoughts so you can overcome that fear of the unknown. No matter how experienced you are, you will face other challenges and setbacks. You must weed the unruly garden of your mind of anything that might choke your best ideas. Host only those mental signals that are supportive and restorative.

Three more suggestions. First, learn to read a profit and loss (P&L) sheet. You'd be shocked to realize how many smart people who have earned their master's in business can't perform this essential task, and physicians rarely know how because financial education is not part of the medical school curriculum. Instead, many doctors buy luxury cars and big houses, then wonder why they feel trapped.

Second, imagine the shape of a funnel. The bottom portion is narrow. This represents the initial money you have for real estate investing. No matter how much you begin with, you want it to expand, but how? Any money you earn from a property goes right back into real estate. Pretax income is powerful because it allows you to buy far more than the taxed income others often use. Remember that you are deferring payment to Uncle Sam, and someday, he'll want his piece of the pie. If you stick to this simple reinvestment plan, your equity will widen and climb. Before you know it, what you began with will be as rotund as the top of the funnel.

Third, as you gain experience, you will develop a multifamily real estate résumé, of sorts. This stellar track record will make it easier for you to win approval for Fannie Mae, Freddie Mae, and loan agencies. By this point, you have nothing to prove. It's the property, not the buyer, that must qualify for the money.

There are methods for using this information and staying on the right path. I've described how I now leverage the time, skill, and experience of my team members. You can and should do the same, even if you don't intend to begin an asset management firm.

Surround yourself with people who are supportive but frank, even if you only intend to make your first multifamily or commercial real estate investment. Avoid know-it-alls and skeptics and focus on people who know more than you or have qualities you admire, attributes that you can put to work for you and your whole team. Be honest about your goal: to better understand how to enter a new realm of passive income investing.

As you proceed, don't overwhelm this circle of supporters with a boatload of requests. Ask for comments or referrals or an objective assessment of your fears, as needed.

Avoid playing ping pong in your mind. We all have thousands of thoughts fighting for attention every day, including your advisors. Isn't it curious, then, that we all seem to think we are so wise about other people's lives, when we have our own to deal with? There is a good reason for this: We're on the outside looking in. Our objectivity, which some would call wisdom, allows us to avoid all the mental gymnastics that may stymie the person asking for help.

This is not to suggest that you surrender to all advice. Merely seek new perspectives. Asking questions may uncover an idea or store of knowledge you were not previously aware of, something that has happened to me many times. As I have already confessed, my mistakes have been my best teachers.

My asset management firm seeks investment properties that range in cost from five and fifteen million dollars. We are a small to medium group, as compared to other firms. Regardless, for me personally, my newest endeavor represents an enormous expansion of my previous involvement.

Your next step may seem tiny as compared to what I am now doing. Don't cripple yourself with those kinds of comparisons. Move forward. Call out the doubtful thoughts that race through your mind and embrace those that make you strong.

## Passive Income Physician takeaways!

- Leverage your circle of friends and colleagues. One idea from each will expand your confidence and knowledge.

- Recognize those moments when you are no longer the boss; do not let yourself be ordered around by a swarm of fearful, ridiculous, paralyzing thoughts.

- One good multifamily or commercial real estate investment can change your portfolio and perspective. Even a dribble of reliable passive income is an inspiration.

# FOURTEEN

# Class Action

Class is a powerful word, one with many connotations. Some consumers accept nothing less than first-class accommodations when traveling, for example. Throughout history, some nations have defined portions of society as upperclass and lowerclass, and you've seen me refer in this book to my middleclass upbringing. Class AAA, also known as Triple-A, is the highest level of play in Minor League Baseball in the United States, and then there is real estate.

Multifamily property classifications—A, B, and C—can reveal a lot to investors, but that doesn't mean we should look down our noses at Class B or C and consider them inferior to Class A. In fact, they may provide a better investment scenario, and there are several reasons why.

For one, they have aged and may lack amenities common to new buildings, so the asking price will be lower.

Second, the need for basic or extensive repairs is exactly what we need to implement forced appreciation methods. By upgrading, we immediately improve the value of the property.

Finally, these multifamily complexes may be adjacent to thriving neighborhoods, which will make them attractive to renters after the upgrades are in place. Of course, the renovations may include the amenities many Class A properties already offer.

Upwardly mobile was once a popular term used to describe people of modest means who wished to improve their standing in society. A piece of property cannot be aspirational, but its owners can. Fixing up a Class B or C property may not raise its classifications, but the loving care will improve its fortune and worth, the monthly revenue it provides the investors.

Age is a defining factor for Class A properties. Usually, Class A indicates that the property has been built within the last ten years, but there are exceptions. Older complexes that have been significantly restored also fit the class, as do high-rise addresses that are twenty years or older but located in urban business centers. In each case, these structures were constructed with high-quality materials, spruced up with quality landscaping, and include remarkable extras, like clubhouses.

They are typically situated in major markets, the best residential neighborhoods, or key urban areas such as financial districts or cultural centers. In short, they are enviable destinations.

Before we leave our discussion of Class A, it is important to mention that there is one more way a building can be considered top tier, even though it lacks the credentials already defined: It commands rent comparable to that of other Class A buildings, even if it exists in what we call a submarket. I've mentioned submarkets once or twice before, but to clarify, this is a small geographical area that is not mainstream but is busy. The people there are in need of basic goods and services, like grocery stores, gas stations, etc. The Fort Worth multifamily complex I doted on earlier is one example, but submarkets vary, depending on the community. Class B properties have been built within the last twenty to thirty years. This means the exterior and interior designs are dated and are, therefore, less attractive than Class A complexes. Other attributes include quality construction that has been maintained through the years. Therefore, the rent is comparable to that of nearby units in this class, which might also be defined as working class.

Class C multifamily structures have been built within the last thirty to forty years. The exteriors and interiors are dated, to be sure, including appliances that are defined as original. These buildings also show their age because maintenance has been deferred, a nice way of saying ignored. You might be tempted to describe these as fixer-uppers, and some serious renovation would improve rent, which falls well below that of Classes A and B. In the end, the lower property classes offer bigger profit margins because they need work. It is fun to improve a property, to give it a makeover and watch it fill with families and individuals who appreciate having a nice place to live. There is one exception though. Class D properties are deeply distressed and exist in downtrodden neighborhoods. Some investors are attracted to these properties; however, this class is beyond the scope of our discussion.

There are no hard and fast rules to help us choose the ventures in which we should invest. Knowing the major market and how the submarkets relate is a good place to begin. We also cannot deny another adage when it comes to real estate: "Location, location, location!" Then there is the issue of timing. If you find an attractive Class C property in an area that is undesirable but close to a thriving market, how long will it take for the fringe to be embraced by good fortune? The next issue is financing. What will the lenders think of your vision? They

> **Knowing the major market and how the submarkets relate is a strong place to begin.**

want to protect and grow their money. To them, Class A assets will look solid, and Class B assets located in or near major markets may be appealing because they will attract young professionals who can afford the rent. More risk naturally causes more concern about return on investment percentages.

I may not have become aware of these factors if I had remained a buyer of single-family homes. Although newer homes were preferable, in the years when I was seeking viable properties, there was a glut. I had plenty to choose from in upper-middle-class neighborhoods, so there was no real debate about which class to choose.

The ballgame changed for me big time when I took a step beyond developer of Longview and owner of commercial and multifamily real estate. Now, I was a co-founder of an asset management company that quickly developed a skill for locating exciting real estate opportunities. Thus, we needed to raise money from investors who would fund new projects. Guess what. They may be every bit as fussy as the banks, with good reason.

As a newbie in real estate, I could not put myself in the position of getting in way over my head. Each step forward required taking a risk, and I only did so after some careful analysis and requesting guidance from my teachers.

Also, when my firm reached out to investors with

PPMs, the group I was most interested in contacting included physicians. I was already keenly aware of the financial beating they take, and I understand the frustration that comes with just trying to get ahead. Once again, though, I was determined to move forward. To do so, I had to provide excellent investment proposals and be willing to consult and educate. I didn't mind. Hey, high standards are classy!

### Passive Income Physician takeaways!

- Never go into an investment blind and don't expect anyone else to.

- Classifications help define groups of real estate, but it is the buyer who most defines the potential for profit.

- Learn what you can, then bring someone along by becoming a teacher and sharing what you know.

# FIFTEEN

# MASS APPEAL: A CAUTIONARY TALE

When you spot a real estate opportunity, creativity kicks in. You have a vision. Transforming a property is a thrill. Just don't expect everybody to share your excitement.

My Longview project was enormously gratifying because I had a hand in nearly every decision that had to be made. That success inspired my partner and me to grab another piece of land in a nearby city and make magic.

Zoning for the three-acre lot we bought was limited to a couple single-family homes, but building two houses didn't make much sense. The interesting aspect of the land was its location. It was situated between a 34-year-old suburb and a townhouse-style apartment complex. We decided to seek a zone variance that would allow us to create thirty-two units in quality multifamily townhouse structures, all of which would be connected. We weren't there to shout, *"There goes the neighborhood!"* Instead, we were merely expanding a type of housing that already existed. Perhaps naïvely, we believed we were improving the area.

We also believed we would succeed because we knew the mayor, city manager, and one member of the City Council. At the very least, we knew we could communicate well with them, and we hoped that would enable us to earn the city's support.

We applied for a permit to increase density with townhouses. When you apply for permission to rezone a property, your idea goes public, and citizens are invited to comment. Maybe my earlier bit about bad publicity doesn't apply here, because that was when the odds of victory began tilting against us.

A wildfire of rumors began. The key phrases were "low rent" housing, which then morphed into the fear-mongering lie, "Drugs will be everywhere!"

It didn't help that residents in the suburban neighborhood adjacent to our property began collecting signatures on a petition to deny our request.

Then, my telephone started ringing. A reporter grabbed hold of the story and wouldn't let go. I never should have given interviews, because my project and my name showed up in black and white in the local paper for at least a couple weeks. In hindsight, I should have asked my lawyer to handle all queries.

Remember when I told you that I've learned from all my mistakes? Now I know that the ability to convey your message in a neutral manner is important, a lesson I won't soon forget.

By the time I went before City Council to plead my case, I had been targeted as the evil doctor developer, cast as the proverbial alien invader who wanted to ruin the city. As I stood before the Council I was actually booed by the residents who packed the chamber.

> **Never underestimate the illogic and power of the madding crowd.**

You might think this was a homeowners-versus-renters issue that blew up in my face. Some home dwellers did protest that two-story townhouses would obstruct their view, and that was fair enough, but the throng also included renters from the apartments across the street from my property. What did they have to lose? Nothing, yet they simply refused to hear the truth: We intended to build quality housing that would upgrade the area. We were not interested in lousy, low-rent units, because we knew we couldn't make money that way. Our complex would attract families, millennials, and professionals of all stripes. We had good intentions, but another lesson I learned was to never underestimate the illogic and power of the madding crowd. Needless to say, I was on the losing end of a three-four Council vote.

City officials were still willing to let us build a couple single-family homes on the lot. In fact, they eventually agreed to rezone to allow four houses. Angry and stressed out, I bought a huge sign and had it installed on my three acres: "Coming Soon! Two-Story Rental Homes." The variance did not restrict me to single-story structures, after all, and I was more than willing to play hardball. It was foolish, of course, because it accomplished nothing. If you believe I won because the city compromised by allowing me to build four homes, you're wrong.

Zoning is tricky. The more the city allowed me to do, the more they demanded of me. A larger project was defined as planned development (PD); therefore, it required me to hire an engineer to draw up plans, a costly task indeed. I had already paid for a feasibility study for my townhouse variance permit that outlined how streets and other needs would be addressed. It also included a drainage plan. Regardless, one of the complaints at the City Council meeting was that drainage issues would harm the area. *Did they even read the plan? No. That would be far too logical.*

It reached the point where my partner and I no longer cared to move ahead. Ironically, we sold the property to one of the most ardent members of the opposition. Perhaps he was only trying to protect his view, and he had every right.

Misery loves company, I guess, because we were

not the only losers in that deal. The one City Council member I knew, who supported the project, was voted out of office in the next election cycle.

What else did I learn from all this? First, development is all about zoning. If you don't know anything about this, I suggest you steer clear of these types of projects. Everything you want to build will be contingent on zoning. Don't think for a minute, no matter how well-intended you might be, that you can do whatever you want. Expect opposition of some sort.

Second, never underestimate the sway of an angry mob. In my experience, it is nearly impossible to reason with protesters en masse. If you have a chance to speak to them individually, another outcome might be possible, but it's almost impossible to negotiate against them when you are so sorely outnumbered.

Third, avoid the D-word. When I mention that I am a real estate investor, some people are curious and want to know more. If you identify yourself as a developer, be ready to duck. It is not that there is anything wrong with wanting to develop. After all, where would our cities and towns be if developers did not create housing and retail projects? Nevertheless, for whatever reason, a negative connotation often comes with the territory.

Go figure, then go find another opportunity.

## Passive Income Physician **takeaways!**

- Intentions can be misinterpreted. Find a neutral, nonthreatening way to convey your mission early on.

- Classic issues such as loss of a beloved view, concerns about increased traffic, and style of development projects are part of the playing field. Be ready for questions.

- Understand the costs of creating engineering plans that will be required for zoning variances. If you pay for the work up front and the project fails, you'll take a loss. Never assume that your project is a done deal until it's a done deal.

SIXTEEN

# LIFE IN STORAGE

People can't live in storage units, but their memorabilia and other belongings can. Many human beings are prone to holding on to things for years and years, even if the items are no longer of use.

Investing in the robust arena of storage facilities enjoys some benefits similar to multifamily complexes, such as recurring monthly payments. This means the concept of forced appreciation is viable. Minor upgrades to the facility and raising rent will immediately add value. There are also some other advantages. Human beings don't dwell in the storage spaces, so you will not have to deal with complaints about broken toilets or other problems. The inanimate objects make no noise, won't call you in the middle of the night, and have nothing to say about their accommodations. This type of relationship sounded refreshing to me after enduring all the name-calling and protests in my zoning variance escapade.

Another advantage is that turnover is not rapid. People tend to choose a unit, move their stuff in, then ignore it for several years. Minimal rotation of tenants makes this a stable business with minimal overhead, maintenance, and operational demands. Even better, banks like this type of real estate and often leverage up to 85 percent of the value to help new owners take possession of the property. Finally, the laws governing this sector tend to favor the landlord. There is not a long eviction process in the event of delinquent payments. After thirty days of nonpayment, the tenant is ousted.

It would be fair to ask why I didn't get into this type of real estate sooner. In my case, I was enthralled with the idea of owning a home, so that was where my education and real estate journey began. My learning curve eventually took me to multifamily because the tax benefits were so glorious.          Fortunately,     the discoveries never stop. My awakening to the stability of storage facilities was largely born out of my mistakes and growing knowledge of what it takes to purchase and manage thriving properties, not to mention the realization that passive income need not be limited to one form of investing.

In fact, by broadening my view of what constitutes a strong real estate deal, I was doing what stockbrokers claim we must do when investing in papers assets: diversifying. If the multifamily market becomes too hot and I'm losing bids, I can begin searching another sector for opportunity.

It is a process though. When I set my mind on owning more storage units, I met with brokers who specialized in that niche. I wanted and needed to know more about the market before I dedicated huge sums of money to it.

The same can be said for other real estate. Commercial light industrial spaces can be profitable, as are small office warehouses. Not every business is operated out of a strip mall or home. Plumbing and utility companies seek buildings that are conducive to their services. Even recreational operations, such as the ever-popular baseball batting cages or indoor driving ranges for golf fans, need real estate that is expansive yet spare.

> If the mind believes in and imagines new revenue, good things begin to happen.

The above examples share a strong common bond: They provide recurring income. To find a new possibility is tantamount to inventing money. If the mind believes in and imagines new revenue, good things begin to happen. Even holding in mind the need to revise and expand my notion of hard asset investments creates an energy. I become more creative and collaborative, I reach out, and, before I know it, I'm being productive in bigger ways. To begin, release your best ideas from that stuffy storage unit called your brain. Life is not meant to be stored away, gathering dust. Then choose a focus on one thing: What interests you? Is there an area of real estate that naturally fits in your wheelhouse, so to speak? Do you already own a building that might create more revenue for you with a little brainstorming?

> **Life is not meant to be stored away gathering dust.**

A physician in Detroit, an acquaintance of a friend, owned the building that housed his family practice. It was a good start. He realized that he had extra space he could rent to other medical professionals, but he didn't stop there. One winter day, the snow plow didn't show up to clear the parking lot and sidewalks, so he decided to create his own version of that service and charge his tenants. This was similar to the add-on we discussed when upgrading a multifamily property. All the Motown doctor did was keep an open mind about services that would expand his monthly income. Simple, simple.

My love of multifamily led me to storage and light industrial facilities. In a sense, they all belonged in the same category, so it wasn't a great leap of faith to get involved. I just couldn't see it in the early years of my real estate career. I wonder what bright ideas will visit me next year and the next.

## *Passive Income Physician* takeaways!

- Passive income is prosaic. Starbucks grew on one simple idea: A daily cup of quality coffee is addictive. Now, the company is amazingly creative in its mission to stay relevant.

- Choose a way to begin, then keep an open mind. Are there related ventures that can expand your income?

- We can't expect to always hit home runs. Get to first base as often as possible. Little steps may lead to a big score.

# SEVENTEEN

# DECREASING RISK

For many professionals, buying a first home is a big deal that comes with risks. The inability to pay the mortgage due to illness or loss of a job could lead to foreclosure. The lack of funds to fix the roof or perform general maintenance and upkeep is another potential pitfall. The mortgage crisis in 2008 shed light on the expectations of homeowners who really could not afford the property, or multiple dwellings, they had purchased.

Yet fulfilling the American Dream, that shimmering mirage in the distance, seemed worth the dangers of ownership.

Now I'm suggesting that you rethink the supposed gains of single-family home ownership and take on even bigger financial responsibilities. Buying multifamily units, storage and light industrial facilities, or even limited-use hotels demands large loans and complex financing strategies that may be frightening. Here is what's interesting though: As bigger risks are embraced, new benefits begin to appear.

Let's start with buying a duplex or fourplex. This might seem like a giant step forward. The irony is that you'll take on more financial risk, because even though you'll have tenants paying your mortgage, you will still be limited to recourse loans. This type of funding allows a lender to seek financial damages if the borrower, you, fails to pay and the asset value is not high enough to offset the loan. That, of course is scary, and it makes ownership of a portfolio of small properties sound untenable.

Another type of loan is available for commercial properties. It is called non-recourse, and here's how it works: To buy a large multifamily complex, you apply for a loan secured by collateral, usually property. If you, the borrower, default on payment, the bank can seize the collateral, but there's a big difference: The lender cannot demand any further compensation, even if the collateral does not cover the full value of the defaulted loan amount.

Default is serious business and not an outcome anyone wants. That said, when venturing into commercial holdings, you are treated differently than the individual or couple who buys a home for their family to live in.

Also, keep in mind that buying duplexes will not

profoundly expand your net worth. Since growth of passive income is our goal, investing in larger properties is not only financially advantageous, it comes with the benefit of non-recourse loans.

To recap: You now know that United States tax laws are partial to commercial real estate investments. The appreciation-versus-depreciation formula can put a lot of non-taxed dollars in your pocket. In my opinion, these funds should be used to buy more real estate so you continue the profitable cycle of reducing taxes and expanding hard assets.

You also know that the risk-averse investor can scale up his or her real estate purchases because non-recourse loans provide advantages not available for recourse loan applicants.

Discovering the incentives of commercial real estate investing reminds me why fear is such a killer. It robs us of the future. If I had not reached for something better for me and my family, I never would have learned about tax law or the various funding possibilities, all of which helped alleviate fear.

This leads to a somewhat simple definition of how to create wealth: Take risks, and rewards will eventually follow.

Risk can also be reduced by working with a team. Either build your own or join an asset management firm and rely on that group. Passive investors are not involved in the operations of the properties, yet

> I used to be a fearful doctor. Book learning was one way to dissipate my reluctance and anxiety. I read voraciously.

they can do very well. The key to success is locating a company that believes in education. Blind investments are the first mistake many physicians make when placing funds with a hedge fund manager. They don't really understand the mechanism, but there is no need to remain in the dark. You deserve sufficient information, so demand an explanation. If it is not forthcoming, move on and find another team to work with.

In that case, these are the hallmarks of a solid company:

- Involved in the operations of real estate.

- Delegates authority to property managers that handle day-to-day operations, rent collection, complaint resolution, maintenance, and repairs.

- Oversees the onsite manager, while developing an operating budget for each property, as well as a capital improvement plan, and an exit strategy.

I used to be a fearful doctor. Book learning was one way to dissipate my reluctance and anxiety, so I read voraciously.

Even better is finding mentors you can trust. TR was an early advisor, and his tutelage was an important rite of passage. To this day, we remain friends. When I moved to Texas, I learned from an assortment of men and woman, many of whom had only informal educations but shared one smarty-pants trait: They savored the breakfast of champions, informed risk.

## *Passive Income Physician* takeaways!

- The purpose of accepting risk is to learn. The answers you crave demand that you step through a curtain of uncertainty.

- "Go big or go home" does not suggest doing stupid things; it means growth is often accompanied by advantages and laws partial to the risk-taker.

- The willingness to educate distinguishes one investment firm from another. An honest management company wants its investors to know the details of risk and profit. Questions that go unanswered may encourage worry.

EIGHTEEN

# SATISFACTION: RETIRING OLD IDEAS

My decision to shake off the limited thinking that shaped my youth started when I embraced new ideas about wealth and how to create it. I quickly realized that I do not have to settle for less. The world is teeming with abundance. We just have to set our sails and go after it.

My urge to evolve doesn't end with money matters. Even the concept of retirement can use some revision. Society still clings to the notion that an adult gladly concludes a career so more time can be spent playing golf, visiting grandchildren, or traveling, but what if you don't have a hobby, extended family, or even a wish to have an ocean of obligation-free, unscheduled time?

> The world is teeming with abundance. We just have to set our sails and go after it.

135

There is no single style or formula for retirement. In fact, new data show that many people who are middle-aged and older prefer to stay active, often in a professional capacity. They want to spend their time with activities that are engrossing and enjoyable to them.

That said, many younger people are exploring the concept of retiring early by arranging extended leaves from their careers so they can explore other interests. A few months or a year in another country or professional environment emboldens them to have it all now, rather than waiting till they are 65.

It is difficult, though, for medical people to revise their daily routines. Many of us believe we must stick with the profession we began with, despite the gnawing anxiety that we may have made the wrong choice. It is difficult to walk away from a medical career that demanded ten grueling years of schooling. Perhaps we fear that if we change course, it will mean we wasted that decade of life. On the contrary, I assure you that nothing is wasted if it helps us see who we are and what we really want. Anybody who can survive the rigor of a medical education and career is well trained to succeed at just about anything.

If you want change, merge into another lane gradually. Doing so may make space for other unexpected emotions: joy, fulfillment, and even relief. These feelings are indicators that something has been missing from your life.

Please don't assume you will have to take a serious pay cut to do something different with your life. Some professionals are needlessly willing to earn less to follow their bliss. I say that we must banish that thought. Less money? Why would that make you happier? You can have it both ways. Rethink your investment strategies so you can eventually afford any number of adjustments to your professional life. Sacrificing part of your annual income to find satisfaction is not wise, recommended, nor mandatory.

> **Rethink your investment strategies so that you can eventually afford any number of adjustments to your professional life.**

We stifle growth when we improve one aspect of life but accept old concepts in another area. Make a list of audacious things you know you can't immediately afford to do. When you feel yourself cringing while merely jotting down an outrageous notion, you're on to something. Stay with it. Underline that idea and, beneath it, list all the things that are holding you back. These might include:

- Responsibility to family
- Professional integrity
- Traits you admire in others but don't fit your agenda

- Belief that you must pay for your pleasures, so you agree to live small

I'm tempted to say that after experiencing these knots of anxiety, just let them go, but you've heard that before, and it is not always so easy. The audacious list at least puts you in touch with the barriers that hold you back from making a change. Acknowledge they exist, then deal with them one at a time.

Next, make another list that trashes the archaic concept of retirement. Turn it on its head. Make it look silly in its present form. Maybe you can't afford to take a year off to pursue other ideas, but by reducing your clinical hours each month, you experience a sense of relief, a new definition of early retirement. Shake down the whole notion of retiring so getting past it is no longer so difficult. It is a false god, in the same way that owning a home is a false definition of achieving the American Dream.

> There is only one dream. Freedom to do what you wish with your time.

There is only one dream: the freedom to do what you wish with your time. Only one thing buys that dream for you: recurring passive income that leads to some measure of wealth.

One more idea. If you know you have no intention of retiring, why work at a job that is damaging your health and wilting your personal relationships? My passion for passive income burns brightly within me because the more I have, the broader my choices become. I don't want to burn out in the medical field, only to discover that I can't quite retire in a fashion that excites me and keeps my family safe. I left a partnership in a medical group only to accept a hospital management position. There will come a day when I'll walk out of my office for the last time, when I'll step away and let someone else take over. Does that mean I'll retire? Don't count on it!

There was a time when my biggest fear was becoming some version of Dr. Desperate. I was terrified that I'd end up angry, understandably exhausted, estranged from my wife and children, and, more to the point, devoid of any viable retirement choices. Sure, there was some money in the bank, because I'd put in my time and earned an annual income many Americans would envy. I was one of those allegedly rich doctors who drive nice cars, live in big homes, and still feel a bit desperate. How could I maintain the grind for an entire career? How could I care for others, yet sacrifice my own health?

Those feelings changed as I transitioned into my real estate career and expanded my net worth, but my new responsibilities only deepened my intimate association with the many desperate doctors in our profession. It hit me hardest when my hospital management position demanded that I fire a good man. It had to be done for the sake of staff and patients, and he would not be the last physician I would let go.

A hospital wants to employ excellent healthcare professionals while also providing a safety net for community members who require treatment. When a doctor no longer communicates in a mature manner with staff and is unkind and impatient with people in need, it is time to part ways. In an attempt to save the career of Dr. Desperate, I invited him into my office and explained that he needed to go through a coaching program. I swore we would do our best to help him become a better provider and teammate. That would include cutting his hours in the emergency room and adding more days between his shifts. We hoped the extra rest would allow him to rejuvenate and return to the hospital refreshed, so he could do a better job.

He was receptive and collegial. I liked him, and knew he was a decent person, even though the complaints about his behavior were excessive and gave me every reason to let him go. For a short time, our program worked. He trained, rested, and made a valiant effort to improve.

Soon, though, the fits of anger returned, heaped upon nurses as well as patients. His care for others was sorely lacking, as was his ability to interpret the responses to his medical suggestions. He was also infuriated when he was called into the hospital late at night for an emergency that turned out to be a false alarm. He always blamed the patients, and he could not accept that as physicians, we must respond, regardless of the eventual outcome, that we must react in an attempt to save a life; otherwise, we are not fulfilling our Hippocratic Oath. In the end, I had to utter those iconic words: "You're fired."

There were others who also could no longer control their emotions. One doctor cursed when he was called to help, and he broke a phone receiver by pounding it against a wall in frustration. He didn't want to be there, so I let him go immediately.

Another was racially insensitive, something that is entirely unacceptable in any profession. We treat human beings, not cultures, nations, or demographics.

When we are exhausted, our threshold of patience, humility, and empathy is lowered. At the same time, physicians cannot expect untrained people to be calm when they are suddenly in a panic about pain. We are trained to recognize symptoms, while the average citizen is not. Even though we can tell when a condition is not life-threatening, we are still expected to put on our best face and assure our patient that all will be well in time.

Dr. Desperate is incapable of accepting this. Instead, he or she says, "I don't kiss asses. I save them."

This type of response is unacceptable at any medical institution, and it was likely unacceptable to Dr. Desperate in his early life, when idealism reigned supreme. That was why it hurt to force them into retirement. They had, in the past, done excellent work and served their communities admirably.

You do not want to be on the receiving end of blunt critiques. You don't want to hear that you are no longer fit to serve and that your anger is out of control. You don't want to be admonished for showing disrespect to people who need medical care and for shaming your colleagues, those highly trained, dedicated professionals who are better suited to the work because early in their careers, they took the steps required to become Dr. Bliss.

Within you are warring factions: desperation versus bliss. By now, you already know the choice I made, a choice I suggest for you. I hope you also know that you are entirely capable of making the right decision and creating a life that includes ample passive income.

My story is not necessarily unique. People from all professions experience revelations and turn a corner into a whole new world. I do not know why I believed that becoming a doctor would satisfy me. Maybe it was to make amends for my poor showing as a high school student. Perhaps I was only trying to prove that I was smart enough to get into medical school and save lives, after flopping on my college entrance SAT exams.

Save your own life, physician. Serve the community for as long as you wish, then serve your own humanity. To be rich is meaningless if you are unhappy. This is an age-old tale: the man or woman who has everything, even a million bucks, yet is miserable because fulfillment is not money.

Wait. Haven't I preached that the power of expansive, massive action as a way to improve net worth?

Yes, but fulfillment is having what you want and need every moment of your adult, professional life. If that means living in a mansion, make it happen. If you are content to exist in another environment, that is also worthy, but only if it is what you truly want and you are able to provide for yourself. Surrendering and accepting a lack of funds because you are unhappy in your current profession is not a solution; that will only lead to disappointment, and you're better than that.

Don't do it my way. Do it yours. That said, I hope my adventures in the transformation from doctor to manager of passive income assets has provided you food for thought, reflection and the urge to do something you know you must do: challenge the outmoded, insufficient notion of retiring with a gold watch. There is no handout at the end of your career. All that awaits you is the sum of your intellect, intuition, and courage to use your earning power to serve your best interests.

When I was still serving in the Navy, I could stand on the stern of a United States warship and look out over the ocean toward the horizon. All I could see was the abundance of the green-blue sea, without any borders or limitations. There were no orders to think small and imagine floating toys in a bathtub.

Yet that is what we do when we are trapped in a predicament that may offer a paycheck but not a life, a job but not a mission, a demand without a purpose.

The passive income physician seizes opportunity where others fear to tread. We yearn for the open seas, the aftermath of disappointment and setback, the certainty that something else is possible, if only we will seek the satisfaction of retiring old limitations and ideas that do not serve professional men and women of extraordinary dedication and talent.

My story is not over, and neither is yours, no matter your age. Take one step toward tomorrow that will make you proud and at peace. I was a poor high school student who could not apply to or expect to be accepted into college. Look at me now. I have proven that the past is dead. The only truly living thing is my ability to perceive and fulfill a many-splendored future.

Walk with me.

### Passive Income Physician takeaways!

- Start now, in any way you can, to build steady, passive income.

- Keep pushing forward by learning more about expanding net worth.

- Don't look back and never fear the future.

# THE PASSIVE INCOME REALITY

I know Dr. Bliss. He is energetic, his enthusiasm for life is infectious, and he is always calm and relaxed. His name is Thomas Black. I can testify to his success because I am his CPA. I handle his personal tax preparation and the accounting and tax planning for some of his businesses, and his aura of confidence and joy is something that simply cannot be faked.

I have also encountered a fair number of professional people who fit the description of Dr. Desperate. These individuals are unhappy with their financial portfolios, and, therefore, their tax returns, yet they refuse to try new methods that could expand their wealth and possibly reduce the distress caused by money matters. When I suggest commercial and multifamily real estate and the legal, valuable tax benefits that come along with them, I often get the same responses:

"I'm a doctor. I'm too busy."

"It's too complicated, and I'm too busy.""I earn good enough money at my job."

"If *I* can't understand it, it is most likely too good to be true."

Or, there's just the plain, old, "No."Even younger professionals, physicians in particular, those you might think would be a little more open-minded, turn me down. In general, they want to do everything by the book, and follow in the footsteps of their mentors. They won't accept that the medical arena and economy have changed significantly over the years. It is true that the old ways are not dead, but it is time we admit that they may require life support.

In a way, I can't blame the next generation of doctors. They grew up in the era of the 2008 mortgage crisis. That monumental event caused a lot of financial damage and meant the ruin of some homeowners who had bought into the Gold Rush-like frenzy of the American Dream, only to be forced to bite the bullet of foreclosure in the end.

Yet here is the irony: Physicians and professionals who were already properly invested in multifamily real estate, for example, weathered the storm quite well and were not pressured to sell at a loss. They had cash flow and pretax dollars at their disposal, which left them plenty with which to buy new properties when valuations plummeted. For many real estate investors, the financial downturn was an amazing opportunity to buy income-earning properties at huge discounts.

Also, their method of creating wealth was not something new, not an invention of the money grabbers of the late 1990s mortgage bubble. Commercial and multifamily real estate have a history of establishing and growing net worth. It is tried and true, with virtues based on evidence.

Meanwhile, the crash of the mortgage market ripped a hole in paper assets, stocks and bonds. Some portfolios that were traded in 401(k) plans—the tax-qualified, defined-contribution pension account defined in subsection 401(k) of the Internal Revenue Code—lost up to 50 percent of their value. Only now, nearly a decade later, are these returning to previous levels. In other words, those investors lost ten years of investment returns in retirement accounts, whereas many real estate investors continued to earn steady passive income and saw their net worth increase substantially. The downfall of stocks had a frightening ripple effect. Some professionals, many in their fifties at the time, were finally fed up. To make up for the sluggish performance of their portfolios, they decided to get more aggressive with paper assets to ensure their retirement plans.

Unfortunately, I have had to stand on the sidelines and witness a virtual train wreck, because this type of investing invariably caused even more financial damage for many. Expressing anger and frustration through an investment account doesn't fix anything. You can't suddenly accelerate, make up for lost time, and earn big profits. Thus, the only ones who managed to get rich were the brokerage firms.

Furthermore, it is leverage that allows us to make a lot of money without risking huge sums. I can think of no better way than real estate to do just that. Yes, stocks can be purchased on margin, and this, too, is leverage, but if that security loses value, your broker will call and legally demand money to cover the loss. In 2008, most margin calls resulted not only in investors being forced to sell their leveraged stock, but many also had to withdraw money from their other accounts to make up for the margin debt that wasn't covered by the sale. Because they were trading on margin, the investors basically had no choice but to sell those assets. If they would have been able to retain the stock investment, they would likely have recovered their money. This illustrates the worst-case scenario when leveraging equity investments, yet that exact thing occurred millions of times in 2008, 2009, and even back at the dawn of this millennium, back in 2000 and 2001.

This is not how it works in commercial real estate, as Tom clearly explains in his chapter about recourse and non-recourse loans. When purchasing an apartment complex, you may put down 20 percent of the value or pool money with other investors. If the bottom falls out, the banks don't come after you and demand more money. They foreclose.

Let's take another look at the doctor who bought stock on margin and, this time, made a profit. This is great, except that he must now pay taxes on 100 percent of that dividend. Meanwhile, the investor in commercial real estate can claim legal tax deductions to offset his profits and operating cash distributions and defer taxation. Now he has the option to do what Tom suggests: to use his tax savings to purchase more passive income real estate.

In the last three to five years, I've worked with dozens of doctors. I've enjoyed addressing their specific needs and helping where I can. Some of my clients are fulfilled just to continue in medicine. "I love this," they tell me. "I'm good at it, and I'm okay with whatever I have at retirement." Others are terribly disappointed that their choice of profession, with all its demands and responsibilities, has not provided a golden parachute—at least not yet anyway.

Then there is Tom. When we meet, he is always happy and eager to share his knowledge and talk strategy. His knows that in five to ten years, he won't have to tend to patients in a stressful emergency room unless he wants to. Even now, thanks to his growing net worth, he can cut back on his clinical hours and enjoy his family and real estate pursuits. In other words, he is no longer just a doctor who serves his community well. Now, he serves himself and his loved ones well, too, because Tom has evolved into a passive income physician. He has successfully turned his physician income into wealth creation.

It really can happen to you. We are dedicated to answering questions and helping professionals overcome a career crisis or improve financial health. Taxation is a key issue in building net worth. Take it seriously now, review it, and study it so that in the years to come any hint of desperation will be replaced with bliss.

Mike Pine, CPA

Pine & Company CPAs, PLLC

Made in the USA
Lexington, KY
25 August 2018